A GO! GIRL GUIDES

MEXIC

A WOMAN'S GUIDE TO TRAVELING IN

Go! Girl Guides: Mexico First Edition
Published by Go! Girl Travel LLC, Tucson, Arizona.
© 2012 All Rights Reserved.

Library of Congress Control Number: 2012945718

Layout, Design, & Illustration:
John H. Clark IV and Alyson Kilday
HOP & JAUNT Creative Agency
www.hopandjaunt.com

Maps Courtesy of:
Mexico Tourism Board
www.visitmexico.com
www.magicofmexico.com

Cover Photo:
Ellen Guill
Guanajuato, Mexico

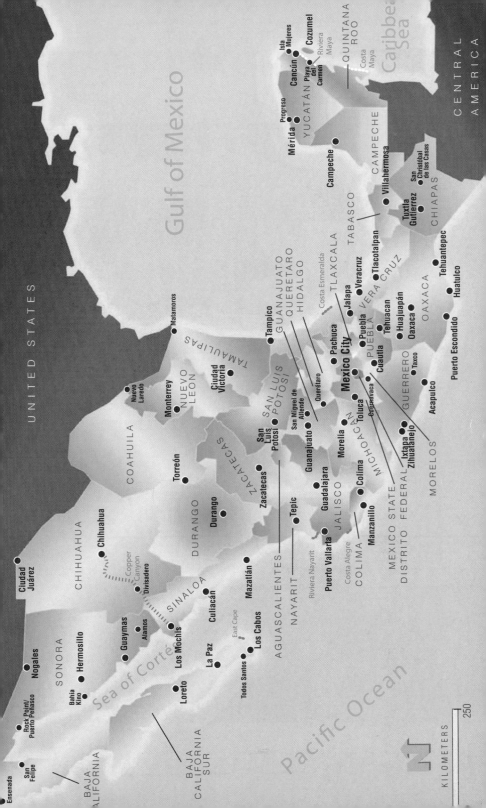

Kelly Lewis, GGG Founder & Editor-in-Chief

Ellen Guill, Author

ABOUT

Go! Girl Guides was created from a dream in early 2011. As seasoned travelers ourselves, we couldn't understand why there weren't resources that addressed the specific needs of solo travelin' gals—so we made one.

In this book, you'll find information that's tailor-made just for you, lady, and we left no stone unturned. You'll get information on safe and inexpensive places to stay, read about common scams to be aware of, find out where to buy tampons and how to get birth control. We want you to stay safe while traveling, and have a blast, too.

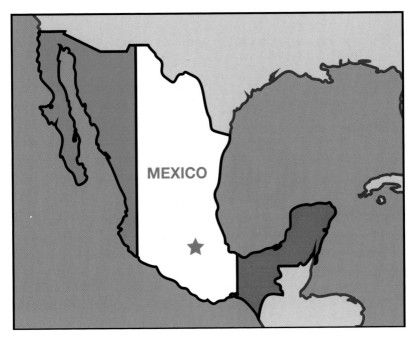

We scoured the country to find the best budget accommodation in the country, and whenever possible, we'll tell you how to get there using public transportation. Primarily, we looked for safety—clean guesthouses and hostels in good neighborhoods, that provide safety deposit boxes, security cameras, key-card access, or have female-only dorms. We saw dozens of ramshackle places that we'd never want to step foot in again ... all so you don't have to.

The world is a very inviting place, and Mexico is no exception.

Get inspired to get out there with first-hand tips from fellow female travelers in our Q&A section, cook up a storm with our Food & Recipe section and find out how to give back during your travels with our Volunteer section, which features only free or low-cost organizations that operate throughout Mexico.

We believe that travel can be both stimulating and affordable.

We believe in adventures that change lives.

We believe that every woman has the power within them to do extraordinary things.

...and we know you do too. So, what are you waiting for?

www.gogirlguides.com

EDITOR-IN-CHIEF
Kelly Lewis
Founder of Go! Girl Guides, Kelly is a writer, a dreamer and an avid traveler. Originally from Hawaii, Kelly lived in New Zealand for a year before traversing through South America and the South Pacific. She started Go! Girl Guides in late 2010 after it came to her in a dream.

AUTHOR
Ellen Guill
Ellen first got the travel bug after spending a semester abroad in Spain. Since then, she has spent two out of the last five years backpacking through Central and South America, Europe and parts of South East Asia. Originally from Los Angeles, Ellen speaks fluent Spanish, and wrote this book while traveling and photographing Mexico solo. She is living proof that you don't need to be afraid to travel on your own through the country. In fact, she loved it so much that she plans to return very soon.

CONTRIBUTORS

Big thank you's go out to editors Chase Gilbert and Justyn Dillingham for catching our stupid mistakes and Hop & Jaunt Creative Agency for their stellar design work. Thank you also to Sam Evans, Maria Balderas, Hot Toddies Unlimited, Alasdair McLeod and Michael Pettet for photos.

A NOTE FROM THE EDITOR

When we first started visiting Mexico back in 2005, we loved it—the people, the beaches, the slow pace of life. It was always a struggle to return to the U.S., and we wore our sunburns proudly.

But then, things in Mexico took a turn for the worse. Narcotics trafficking and related violence began to boom, the media focused largely on the negative issues concerning Mexico, and for a long time we were afraid to return.

With this book, we hope to show you that Mexico is still a safe and beautiful country so long as you stick to the right areas and use caution. You may notice that this book is missing large pieces of the country, and that we chose to focus largely on southern Mexico. Why? Well, we weren't about to send our single female writer into conflict zones in the north, and we certainly can't recommend that you visit those areas right now either.

It's important to remember that the south of Mexico is still largely safe. From ancient ruins to crystal blue seas and lush, tropical jungle, there's an abundance of beauty to be found in Mexico, all for your enjoyment.

We hope you use this guidebook as a way to feel more confident in traveling through Mexico. Use it as a resource, a jumping-off point for planning your adventures, or a way to reassure yourself that your trip will indeed be amazing.

Mexico is a beautiful country. Use common sense, stick to safe areas, ask other travelers for recommendations, and you'll fall in love with Mexico just like we have.

--Kelly Lewis, Editor-in-Chief

CONTENTS

SAFETY

TRAVELING SOLO DOES NOT MEAN YOU'RE ALONE

Why are so many of our well-meaning friends, family and acquaintances opposed to the idea of a woman traveling alone? They think it's dangerous or lonely. They ask you how you plan to meet people, where you'll go, and what you will do by yourself in a foreign country. There are also your own apprehensions about traveling solo - safety, money, friends, family, fear. But everything at home will be just as you left it when you get back. And the fear about staying safe, well, we're here to alleviate that for you.

You're an adult. You are not a vulnerable girl who can't take care of yourself. You've been doing just fine, we're assuming, paying bills, working hard and making your own decisions wherever it is you call home. So what's the great risk in doing the exact same thing in another location? As far as we can see, there isn't one.

Photo courtesy of Hot Toddies Unlimited

If you think of your solo trip as a grand adventure, on which you can do whatever you want, wherever you want, an opportunity to explore another country on your own terms and schedule, you've come up with a win-win. And the best thing about traveling alone is that you don't have to answer or cater to anyone but yourself. Read, wander, take photos, speak Spanish, do nothing for an entire day except lounge in a hammock on a quiet beach, see a whole city in another. Why not? Never try, never know.

If you're worried about meeting people, don't be. You'll meet people in hostels, on the street, in cafes and restaurants, on buses and planes, through friends and fellow travelers. You'll run into people you've met before in a completely different part of the country. You'll explore. Dream. Discover. The backpacker community is, by in large, friendly and open. Plus there are a few, useful online forums to help you get started:

Couchsurfing.org
Make plans to check out the community meetings in your city of choice, find a place to crash, connect with some cool locals or just post your travel itinerary in a group discussion and see if anyone wants to join you – and they probably will!

Facebook
Ask your buddies on Facebook if they have any friends on your route you can meet up with. Chances are, at least one person has family, friends and even a few recommendations for you. Follow up, and don't forget to say thank you!

The most important thing you can do to ensure you meet people? Be open. Talk to people around you. Smile and say hello to those in your hostel, on your bus or plane. Ask them their plans for the day, where they're from, where they've been, where they're going. Other travelers are your greatest resource while on the road, and with any luck, your new friends.

TIPS ON HOW TO STAY SAFE AND USE COMMON SENSE ON THE ROAD

These basic tips will help you navigate Mexico safely, and the rest of the world:

Don't Get Drunk
Feel free to enjoy yourself and indulge a little bit, but don't get too crazy. You'll be tempted to drink a lot in Mexico – beers on the beach, in the street, at dinner, in the hostel, maybe even a *michelada* or *cielo rojo* with breakfast to kill your hangover. But getting so drunk that you aren't aware of what's going on, can't remember how you got home or what you did is a bad idea - a very, very bad idea. The best way to stay safe is to stay alert and aware of where you are and what's going on around you. So go ahead and have a few, but not so many that you become a sloppy, easy target. Cool?

Avoid Drugs
Drugs are a major reason why parts of Mexico are unsafe at the moment, and when you buy drugs in Mexico, you're contributing to an underground drug trafficking trade that is responsible for thousands of deaths a year. On top of that, drugs are the easiest way to ensure you are not in control of your actions and decisions, lowering your inhibitions and overall ability to stay safe. Don't do drugs!

Learn and Speak Spanish
There are many places where you don't necessarily need to speak Spanish, but other places where it will be very hard to get around without it. Speaking Spanish can only help you. You'll be able to talk to locals and get involved in conversations, learn about culture without needing a translator, effectively negotiate in markets, read menus in restaurants, get directions if you're lost, ask for recommendations, easily get around cities and towns and earn some respect from locals with your language skills. If you're looking to get off the backpacker trail and have some adventures, Spanish is the key.

Stay Off The Beaches at Night
Always. Without exception. This is the golden rule that should stay with you throughout your travels around the world. Generally, beaches are unsafe at night, especially if you're alone. They are not patrolled in Mexico, so save your beach time for daylight hours.

Be Cautious of the Police

Unfortunately, Mexican police are not always on your side. Try to limit your interactions with local police to keep yourself out of trouble. If you have a serious issue, we recommend talking to your hostel staff or someone you trust about it first, then contacting the nearest embassy for advice on how to proceed.

Walk With Purpose

If you take a wrong turn and feel unsafe in a particular neighborhood, walk with purpose towards a business or hotel to ask for directions. Stay alert without seeming paranoid, and walk at a steady pace with a serious, yet calm expression. Act like you know where you're going even if you don't. Take off your head-phones if you're listening to music. Make sure your purse or bag is zipped shut and close to your body. It's important to remember that the people of Mexico are generally warm, helpful, and not out to get you, but listen to your instincts if you feel unsafe and ask for help.

Don't Flaunt It

Wearing flashy, gaudy or expensive jewelry is a no-no, as is overly revealing clothing. As a foreigner, you most likely stand out already, and you don't want to attract unwanted attention, especially in big cities and inland communities. The best way to avoid this is to lower your profile: dress conservatively and keep your accessories to a minimum, unless it's jewelry you've bought locally.

Exception: when you're on the beach – feel free to wear whatever you want! Everyone else is.

Go With Your Gut

Feel uncomfortable or uneasy in a particular situation? Always listen to your gut instinct. You're in charge of whom you spend your time with, how much you reveal about yourself, where you go and how you get there. Remember that a direct, but polite "no, thank you" is always in your realm of possibility.

Practice Humility
There is a diverse class system in Mexico. One of the richest men in the world is Mexican, but there are millions of other people from low socio-economic backgrounds. You will get asked for money on the streets, in plazas, on the beach and even in restaurants by children, men, women, vendors and the elderly. Give a few pesos every once in a while if you can afford it. Be polite when you say "no, gracias" to those who want to sell you something, unless you want to buy it, of course. Remember that many Mexican communities survive on tourism and your generosity. Be humble.

Keep in Touch at Home
Call your family each time you touch down in a new town or city to let them know you're safe. If you plan to stay in one spot for an extended period of time, check in at least once a week. Internet is available practically everywhere in Mexico, so you'll always be able to Skype, and your family will appreciate it. We promise.

Ignore Catcalls
As a solo female traveler, you may run into some *machismo* during your travels from men, such as catcalls or whistles. Uncomfortable? Yes, but almost always harmless. It's best to ignore advances and continue on your way (walking with purpose, of course), but if you feel threatened at any time, head into a business or store and ask for help, or to wait for them to pass. It's also important to note that the people of Mexico are quite friendly, and what you initially think is a catcall could be a simple question from a man – the time, where you're from, a helpful suggestion if you appear lost, or an invitation to have a conversation. We encountered this a lot, especially in the Yucatan.

Some useful phrases if you get stuck:

A forceful '*no*.'

"*Dejame en paz*." Leave me in peace.

"*Basta*." Enough.

"*No me toques*." Don't touch me.

Just for the record, we never had to use any of these phrases during our travels, but it's always best to be prepared.

When Asking For Directions, Get a Few Opinions

For whatever reason, when asking for directions on the street, sometimes people will tell you they know the place you're looking for even if they don't. Our best guess as to why this is is simply because they don't want to say no – the people of Mexico are that polite. Always walk a block and ask again. It's not that locals purposefully try to steer you the wrong way – most of the time, they're happy to help – but if someone seems unsure, it's likely you're not going to find your destination off their directions. Get a few responses before heading very far.

TIPS FOR RIDING THE BUS

Mexico is a huge country, and the easiest and most economical way to see it is by bus. Here are some tips for the ride:

Take The First Class Bus

They're more expensive than second-class buses, but are definitely the most safe and comfortable option, with reclining seats, air conditioning, bathrooms on board, TVs and direct trips between locations. First class buses are almost always available, depending on your destination, and all major companies have websites so you can check departure times, arrival times and cost of the trip before you go. Some popular companies are ADO, Primera Plus, TAP and ETN.

Sit At The Front

You get to select your seat when you purchase your ticket - pick one in the front of the bus. This keeps you as far away from the bathrooms as possible, and it ensures you're close to the driver in case you should need help for any reason.

Carry on the Important Stuff

Bring a small bag or backpack on board with your valuables – laptop, electronics, credit cards, passport, cash, jewelry, etc. Keep this with you at all times. It's also a good idea to wear a money belt – this makes theft both harder and less likely.

Bring an Extra Layer

The air conditioning on-board seems to be on high at all times. Make sure to wear warm clothes for your journey, no matter how hot it is outside (socks and closed-toed shoes, pants, layers on top).

If It's Around A Holiday, Buy Your Tickets in Advance
Buses will fill up around the holidays. Buy your tickets a few days in advance, especially if you're heading from the city to the coast.

Pack Food and Water
You're not fed on the buses, and food options at bus stations are limited. Eat a meal before you get onboard if you're traveling a long way. Bring snacks and water. Food vendors may be allowed on board if your bus makes stops, but don't count on this. Think ahead.

Don't Arrive Anywhere Unfamiliar at Night
Sometimes it's unavoidable, but it's much easier and safer to arrive in a new place during the day.

Do Some Research Before You Get There
Decide where you're going to stay before you leave. Write down the address and the cross street. Find out what the best way to get there is from the bus station or airport. Can you walk? Is there a local bus that will take you? Does the hostel offer a shuttle service? How much should a taxi cost? And the most important question – do they have a bed available? All of these questions should be answered before you arrive and this guidebook will help you. Call ahead.

Tend to Get Motion Sickness?
Stop into a pharmacy before you leave and ask for anti-nausea and vomiting pills, or "*pastillas contra el nauseas y vomito.*" *Dimenhidrinato* works like a charm. Take one pill 30 minutes before you board.

·········· HOW TO PROTECT YOUR BELONGINGS ··········

Staying in shared hostel rooms, traveling by bus, taking public transportation and walking through crowds with valuables can be somewhat nerve-racking if you're not prepared. Here are some tips on keeping your belongings safe:

• Stay in hostels with lockers and pack a small lock. Use it everywhere you stay to lock up your valuables. If something doesn't fit in your locker, store it out of sight, like under your pillow, or between the sheets.

- Only leave electronics to charge when you're in the room.

- Split up large sums of money into different compartments of your carry on and backpack. That way, if someone comes upon some pesos, it won't be all of them. When traveling between destinations, wear a money belt and keep your passport, credit cards, and the majority of your cash inside.

- Your purse or day-bag should have a zipper. The most practical bags can be worn cross-body. Keep your bag in front of your person and zipped shut. Be aware of where it hangs when you are on public transportation and walking through large crowds.

- When traveling on buses, keep your carry-on bag on your lap or in front of your feet. There are overhead spaces for storage, but keeping it in your line of sight makes it harder to take.

Don't be paranoid - be cautious! Common sense is the most powerful weapon you have against theft.

MODESTY IS THE BEST POLICY

Wondering how to dress in Mexico? You'll likely have the best experience if you cover up a bit. This is particularly important when in cathedrals, churches and other religious sites. It's also a good idea to dress on the conservative side while you are in Mexico to avoid unwanted male attention.

Exception: When on the beach or in beach towns, it's acceptable to dress as you would during hot months at home. Bikinis, sarongs, shorts, and crop tops are common.

COMMON SCAMS AND HOW TO AVOID THEM

Pickpockets
Around the world, the pickpocket is the easiest way to come up on cash, phones, electronics and whatever else is within easy reach of a distracted target. The best way to avoid getting pickpocketed is to keep your bag in front of your body, zipped shut. When walking through dense crowds or packed public transportation, keep your free hand over the zipper and your gaze alert.

Pickpockets are usually not seen or heard, and the easiest targets are the ones who are not paying attention.

Purses with interior compartments are also a great way to prevent pickpockets. The harder it is to get to your cash, camera, phone, etc., the less likely it is that anything will be stolen.

The Slashed Bag

In bigger cities around large, crowded tourists attractions (think the Zocalo on a Sunday), unsuspecting people sometimes have their purses cut open by an anonymous thief standing behind them. Once the hole is cut, everything inside is on the ground and snatched up. The best way to avoid this is to carry your bag in front of your body and hold it there until you're away from the crowd. The easiest bags to cut are made out of cloth, so consider something more sturdy, like leather, if you're planning a big day of sightseeing.

Taxi Driver Taking You for a "Ride"

Street taxis in Mexico City are notorious for this one, and it's hard to avoid unless you know where you're going and the route to get there. Since taxis use meters, they opt to take you on a "ride" instead of the direct route, ensuring a higher fare. Irritating, yes, but not life-threatening.

Ask your hostel staff the general route before taking a taxi, and tell the driver which way you'd like to go. Or you can also ask your hostel to call you a secure taxi and pay a flat rate instead. The trouble with the secure taxis is they're usually much more expensive than a regular ride, but are also trustworthy. The choice is yours.

"That Hostel is Full"

Some taxi drivers get commission for taking passengers to specific hostels or hotels. So instead of taking you to the hostel where you have a reservation, they insist it's booked solid and try and take you to another. If you've called ahead (which you should have, if you read the earlier sections), you'll know this is not true. If they refuse to take you where you want to go, simply exit the taxi and wait for another. (For the record, this never happened to us while in Mexico).

"Official" Taxis in Bus Terminals and Airports

Marked stations inside the Mexico City bus terminals and international airports sell tickets for secure taxis. The rate is fixed and depends on your destination. Non-secure taxis are outside terminals and have hustlers inside the building looking to recruit travelers, insisting they are fair and safe. They will almost always rip you off. Wait in line and buy a ticket.

WATER SAFETY

Some of the biggest waves in the world hit Mexican coast-lines, the most famous in Puerto Escondido at Zicatela beach. Professional surfers come annually to test their skill here, and spend years learning how to read the ocean. The sea is a serious force of currents, tides, sets, marine life and reefs, and commands respect.

We're not trying to scare you. In fact, many places along the Pacific and Caribbean are calm and are great places to swim. But the ocean can change quickly. Small waves become big, currents change direction and winds pick up. Here are some tips if you run into trouble:

- Don't swim right after a big meal or if you've been drinking. Wait for 30 minutes, just like mama said, so you don't cramp up.

- Observe the ocean for five to 10 minutes before running in. Notice how big the waves are and which direction swimmers who are already in the water drift. When the waves calm down and there's an opportunity to jump in, go for it.

- If you feel a current pulling you out to sea, do your best not to panic and go with it. In a fight between you and the ocean, the ocean will always win, and you'll wear yourself out in the process. Tread water and wait for the current to start pushing back towards land, then swim to shore. Catching a wave is the easiest way to do this. Start swimming as the wave forms and ride it to where you can stand.

- If you ever get caught out in a big swell or a shore break and a wave is going to break right in front of you or on top of you, swim to the bottom of the ocean with your hands in front of your face and grab the sand. The bigger the wave, the deeper you need to go.

STATES AND AREAS TO AVOID

The U.S. State Department issued an updated travel warning in February, 2012, for tourists planning to visit Mexico, including state-by-state and city-specific assessments regarding crime and violence. Rodolfo Lopez-Negrete, Chief Operating Officer for the Mexico Tourism Board, was quoted in the *Los Angeles Times* with this travel update:

> *"The Mexico Tourism Board has long advocated for travel advisories which abide by three key tenets: context, clarity and specificity. The revised U.S. State Department travel advisory regarding Mexico adheres to these principles and should serve as a model for the rest of the world."*

The U.S. State Department lists the following states and cities in Mexico as ones to avoid at the moment, unless necessary:

Northern Mexico

- **Northern Baja California**, especially Tijuana.
- **Chihuahua:** Especially Ciudad Juarez, which has one of the highest murder rates in Mexico.
- **Coahuila**
- **Durango**
- **Nuevo Leon:** The metropolis of Monterrey is listed as an acceptable place to visit, although we heard differently throughout our travels. Avoid Nuevo Leon.
- **San Luis Potosi,** except the city of San Luis Potosi.
- **Sinaloa:** Mazatlan is the major tourist attraction in Sinaloa, and is considered acceptable to visit. The warning does specify exercising caution in Mazatlan during late hours of the night and early morning.
- **Sonora**
- **Tamaulipas**
- **Zacatecas**

Southern Mexico

- **Aguascalientes**
- **Colima**
- **Guerrero:** Acapulco, Ixtapa and Zihuatanejo are considered safe to visit. People continue to flock to Acapulco, but use caution when visiting.
- **Jalisco:** Avoid Jalisco's borders with Michoacan and Zacatecas. Guadalajara and Puerto Vallarta are safe to visit.
- **Michoacan:** Morelia and Lazaro Cardenas are listed as acceptable to visit.
- **Morelos**
- **Nayarit:** North of the city of Tepic is considered dangerous. Riveria Nayarit and the southern part of the state are considered safe to visit.
- **Veracruz**

⋯⋯ MURDERS OF WOMEN IN CIUDAD JUAREZ ⋯⋯

Please do not cross the border into Ciudad Juarez right now. The town, which borders El Paso, Texas, has exploded with violence in recent years, and much of that violence has been against women—so much so, that the term *"femicide"* or *"feminicide,"* defined as "the killing of females by males because they are females," has been used to refer to the rape, mutilation, and murder of thousands of girls and women in the area since 1993.

Due to an inadequate judicial system and a corrupt police force investigating these murders, most of the homicides go unsolved, and as such, there is no way to give a proper estimate to the number of the dead. But, according to Amnesty International, over 300 women were murdered in Juarez in 2011 alone.

Most of the victims come from impoverished backgrounds and work as students, waitresses or in factories. The murder rate for females in Juarez is less than the murder rate for males, but the statistics of female homicides per capita in Juarez is significantly higher than any other major city in Mexico or the United States. Criminal gangs that operate in extortion and kidnapping do so with near impunity.

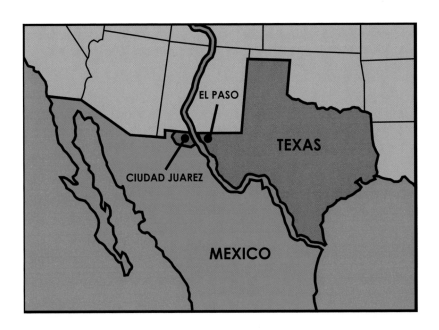

SAFE STATES TO VISIT

The following states are listed with no advisories in effect, meaning they are considered safe to visit. Because we want you to have an amazing time in Mexico, we largely focused the information on this guidebook on these states.

- **Southern Baja California:** Including Cabo San Lucas, San Jose del Cabo, Todos Santos and La Paz.
- **Campeche**
- **Chiapas**
- **Mexico City**
- **Guanajuato**
- **Hidalgo**
- **Southern Portion of Nayarit**, including Riviera Nayarit.
- **Oaxaca**
- **Puebla**
- **Queretaro**
- **Quintana Roo**
- **Tabasco**
- **Tlaxcala**
- **Yucatan**

FAST FACTS FROM THE U.S. STATE DEPARTMENT

- Millions of U.S. citizens safely visit Mexico each year for study, tourism and business, including for more than 150,000 who cross the border every day.

- The Mexican government makes considerable efforts to protect foreign citizens and there is no evidence that criminal organizations in Mexico have targeted U.S. visitors or residents based on their nationality.

- Since 2006, 47,515 people have been killed in what the Mexican government calls narcotics-related homicides. Of those people, 120 were U.S. citizens. That's about .003 percent.

- If you steer clear of northern Mexico and the other states listed in the travel warning, use common sense, and don't participate in any sort of drugs or illegal activity, the odds are that the only thing threatening you in Mexico is sun exposure.

For more information, visit travel.state.gov

U.S. EMBASSIES

Here is a list of some of the U.S. Embassies located throughout Mexico. For a complete list, visit usembassy.gov.

In case of emergency, call the embassy closest to you, press zero, and ask the operator to transfer you to the duty officer.

Mexico City
Paseo de la Reforma 305
Colonia Cuahtemoc
06500 Mexico, D.F.
Within Mexico: +01 555-080-2000
From the U.S.: +011 52 555-080-2000
www.mexico.usembassy.gov

Guadalajara
Progreso 175
Col. Americana
Guadalajara, Jalisco, Mexico
C.P. 44160
Within Mexico: +01 333-268-2100
From the U.S.: +011 52 333-268-2100
www.guadalajara.usconsulate.gov

Merida
Calle 60 Number 338-K (between streets 29 and 31)
Colonia Alcala Martin
Merida, Yucatan, Mexico 97050
Within Mexico: +01 999-942-5700
From the U.S.: +011 52 999-942-5700
meridacons@state.gov
www.merida.usconsulate.gov

Puerto Vallarta
Paseo de los Cocoteros #85
Sur Paradise Plaza
Interior Local L-7
Nuevo Vallarta, Nayarit
C.P. 63732
Within Mexico: +01 322-222-0069
From the U.S.: +011 52 322-222-0069
consularagentpvr@prodigy.net.mx
www.guadalajara.usconsulate.gov

Tijuana
Paseo de las Culturas s/n
Mesa de Otay
Delegacion Centenario C.P. 22425
Tijuana, Baja California
From the U.S.: +011 52 664-977-2000
acstijuana@state.gov
www.tijuana.usconsulate.gov

Los Cabos
Tiendas de Palmilla, Carretera Transpeninsular Km 27.5
Local B221, San Jose del Cabo, Baja California Sur, C.P. 23406
From the U.S.: +011 52 624-143-3566
usconsulcabo@yahoo.com
www.tijuana.usconsulate.gov

U.S. CONSULATES

The following U.S. consulates mainly serve their cities:

Acapulco: *Hotel Emporio, Costera Miguel Aleman 121 – Suite 14; telephone +011 52 744-481-0100 or +011 52 744-484-0300.*

Cancun: *Blvd. Kukulcan Km 13 ZH Torre La Europea, Despacho 301 Cancun, Quintana Roo, Mexico C.P. 77500; telephone +011 52 998-883-0272.*

Cozumel: *Plaza Villa Mar en El Centro, Plaza Principal, (Parque Juárez between Melgar and 5th Ave.) 2nd floor, Locales #8 and 9; telephone +011 52 987-872-4574.*

Ixtapa/Zihuatanejo: *Hotel Fontan, Blvd. Ixtapa; telephone +011 52 755-553-2100.*

Mazatlan: *Hotel Playa Mazatlán, Playa Gaviotas 202, Zona Dorada; telephone +011 52 669-916-5889.*

Oaxaca: *Macedonio Alcala No. 407, Interior 20; telephone +011 52 951-514-3054 or +011 52 951-516-2853.*

Piedras Negras: *Abasolo 211, Local 3, Col. Centro; telephone +011 52 878-782-5586 or +011 52 878-782-8664.*

Playa del Carmen: *The Palapa, Calle 1 Sur, between Avenida 15 and Avenida 20; telephone +011 52 984-873-0303.*

Reynosa: *Calle Emilio Portes Gil #703, Col. Prado Sur; telephone: +011 52 899-921-6530.*

San Luis Potosi: *Edificio "Las Terrazas", Avenida Venustiano Carranza 2076-41, Col. Polanco; telephone +011 52 444-811-7802 or +011 52 444-811-7803.*

San Miguel de Allende: *Centro Comercial La Luciernaga, Libramiento Manuel Zavala (Pepe KBZON), telephone +011 52 415-152-2357.*

HEALTH

Baja California

Hispano Americano Medical Group
Av Reforma No. 1000 y Calle B
21100 Mexicali, Baja California, Mexico
from overseas: +011 52 686-552-2300
from Mexico: 686-552-2300

Monterrey

Hospital San Jose Tec de Monterrey
Av. Ignacio Morones Prieto No. 3000 Pte. Col. Los Doctores.
CP 64710 Monterrey, Nuevo León, México
from the U.S.: 1-866-475-6334
from overseas: +011 866-475-6334; +011 52 818-389-8390
from Mexico: 81-8389-8390; 818-347-1011

Hospital Santa Engracia (Hospital CIMA Monterrey)
Frida Kahlo 180, San Pedro Garza Garcia,
66260 Nuevo León, Mexico
from the U.S.: 866-540-3382
from overseas: +011 52 818-836-8777; +011 52 866-540-3382
from Mexico: 818-836-8777
www.cimamonterrey.com

Puerto Vallarta

San Javier Marina Hospital
Blvd. Francisco Medina Ascencio #2760
Zona Hotelera Norte
Puerto Vallarta, Jalisco Mexico
CP. 48333
from overseas: +011 52 322-226-1000; +011 52 322-226-1010
from Mexico: 322-226-1000; 322-226-1010

Mexicali

Hospital de la Familia
Circuito Brasil 82
Parque Industrial El Alamo
Mexicali, BC México 21210
from the U.S.: +011 52 866-961-1833; +011 52 619-247-6824
from Mexico: 686-565-7555

Guadalajara

San Javier Hospital
Av. Pablo Casals 640 Col. Prados Providencia Esq. con Eulogio Parra
Guadalajara, Jal. México
C.P. 44670
from overseas: +011 52 333-669-0222
from Mexico: 333-669-0222

Hospital Country 2000
Av. Jorge Alvarez del Castillo No. 1542 Chapultepec Country C.P. 44610
Guadalajara, Jalisco, Mexico
from overseas: +011 52 333-854-4500
from Mexico: 1-800-627-5885; 333-854-4500

Centro Medico Puerta de Hierro
Boulevard Puerta de Hierro 5150,
Col. Puerta de Hierro. Guadalajara,
Jalisco México 45116
from overseas: +011 52 333-848-2158; (+01) 619-878-2732
from Mexico: 01-333-848-2100; 01-333-848-4000

Tijuana

Hospital Angeles
Av. Paseo de los Héroes #10999
Zona Río Tijuana C.P. 22010
Tijuana, B.C. México
from overseas: +011 52 664-635-1800; +011 52 664-635-1900
from Mexico: 664-635-1800; 664-635-1900

ENDING A PREGNANCY

Legal termination of a pregnancy is only available in the federal district of Mexico City. Any woman may voluntarily decide to terminate a pregnancy within the first trimester, or first 12 weeks of a pregnancy, in this part of Mexico. The reform to the Robles Law, which includes a woman's right to choose, was passed in April, 2007, and deemed constitutional by the Mexican Supreme Court in August 2008.

Mexican federal law states that if a woman is a victim of sexual violence, emergency contraception must be offered to the victim, and if pregnancy results from a rape, health personnel must give the woman information, counseling and access to legal termination of a pregnancy. Abortion of pregnancy from a rape is legal in all states of Mexico. For more information, visit *www.gire.org.mx*.

Angelica Garcia Olivares, Psychologist, MexFam

BIRTH CONTROL AND HOW TO GET IT

Birth Control
You can get birth control in Mexico, but it will be difficult, if not impossible, to find the same brand that you take regularly at home. Bring enough to last the length of your trip, if possible, and keep the packet of information that comes with your prescription at home to show a pharmacist to find a close match.

Morning After Pill (Plan B)
Emergency contraception, or the morning after pill, is available for purchase at pharmacies throughout Mexico. Simply walk

into a pharmacy and ask the pharmacist for the "*pastilla del dia despues*" (translated: the day after pill).

Condoms

Condoms are widely available, and you can always buy them at any local pharmacy, but they are more expensive in Mexico than they are in the U.S. For peace of mind, bring condoms from home with you. Make sure they are not expired and in good condition. It's always best to be prepared—practice safe sex both at home and while traveling.

··· FEMININE HYGIENE PRODUCTS YOU SHOULD ··· BRING FROM HOME

Tampons

Bring enough for your first cycle. You can find tampons in pharmacies, corner stores and even grocery stores throughout Mexico, with the exception of Chiapas and Oaxaca, where they can be hard to find.

Any other medications

Do you take any other medications regularly? Bring enough of each to last the length of your stay.

····· VACCINATIONS AND REQUIRED MEDICINE ·····

Your before-you-go checklist should include a doctor's visit, approximately 4–6 weeks prior to your departure. According to the U.S. Center for Disease Control, recommended vaccinations for Mexico include:

- Routine vaccinations, including measles, mumps, tetanus shot
- Hepatitis A
- Hepatitis B
- Typhoid

Also recommended: Malaria. Incidences of Malaria are present in the states of Chiapas, rural areas of Nayarit, Oaxaca and Sinaloa. A few, rare cases have been reported in Quintana Roo, Tabasco, Chihuahua, Durango and Sonora. If you plan to visit these areas of Mexico, talk to your doctor about getting Malaria medicine and the risks involved.

A GUIDE TO NAVIGATING A MEXICAN PHARMACY

Mexican pharmacies are pretty straightforward. They are located throughout the country, and inside you can buy everything from shampoo to the morning after pill, and any other medicine you need, as long as you know how to ask for it.

Pharmacists don't always speak English, and unless you know the medicinal name for the prescription you're seeking, you'll have to describe your symptoms or what you're looking for to the pharmacist behind the counter. More often than not, you'll need to have these conversations in Spanish, so come prepared – look up translations online for the symptoms you're experiencing, or ask your hostel staff if they know the name of the medicine you're seeking.

Some common women's health medicines, and how to ask for them:

Morning After Pill:
Pastilla del dia despues

Yeast Infection:
Diflucan (prescription). Saying "*Monistat*" usually does the trick.

Bacterial Infection:
We're not sure of the official name, but the translation for this one is '*infeccion bacterial.*'

Rehydration Medicine:
'*Medicina para la rehydracion*'

Anti-nausea/Seasick medicine:
Pastillas en contra de la nausea y vomito

Tips to Avoid Malaria

Use insect repellant with Deet and apply it multiple times a day. Wear long pants and shirts with long sleeves to prevent mosquito bites.

Sleep in closed, air-conditioned spaces with mosquito nets or bed tents.

Take regular prescription malaria drugs, if recommended by your doctor.

Q&A

WITH A WOMEN'S HEALTH DOCTOR

DR. VICENTE DIAZ
Deputy Director,
International Planned
Parenthood Federation/
Western Hemisphere Region

Dr. Diaz is the Deputy Director for IPPF/WHR, and is also the former director of MexFam, an organization that provides family planning services throughout Mexico. Here, he shares with us important information every woman should read before traveling to Mexico.

What do you think women need to keep in mind while traveling to Mexico?

Mexico is an incredibly diverse country with many variances in terms of income, accessibility and culture. There are some communities that are very conservative, for example, while others are very liberal in terms of ideas and behavior.

What sorts of female health issues do you think female travelers should be aware of while in country?

Mexico is considered a middle income country, and is now mostly urban. Public health coverage is nearly universal. Health issues affecting young people are related mostly to violence and traffic accidents.

Is contraception widely available?

Contraceptive methods are available without a prescription in nearly all pharmacies in the country. Family planning services, including contraception, are provided free of charge through the Ministry of Health. Non-profit organizations such as International Planned Parenthood affiliate MEXFAM A.C. (www.mexfam.org.mx) provide sexual and reproductive health services at a very low cost through a network of clinics throughout the country.

We've heard that it is legal to terminate a pregnancy in Mexico City. Is this true? If so, what are the requirements? Are there several places in Mexico City to visit for this service?

In April 2007, Mexico City's Legislative Assembly legalized abortion during the first 12 weeks of pregnancy. The legal reforms also give priority to sexual and reproductive health care and establish that "related services must be provided in a way so that every person can exercise their right to decide freely, responsibly and in an informed manner on the number and spacing of their children." Outside of Mexico City, abortion laws vary depending on the state, but are generally very restrictive.

Abortion services are provided by the Mexico City Ministry of Health free of charge to all women living in Mexico City, and are available for a small fee to women living outside the city. The private and social sectors can also provide abortion services if they comply with Ministry of Health regulations and standards of care. At least two social organizations—MEXFAM (www.mexfam. org.mx) and Marie Stopes Mexico (www.mariestopes.org.mx) —provide these services for varying fees.

Are there women's clinics within Mexico? How should women find a gynecologist should they need one?

Yes, there are clinics operated by the private, public and social service sectors. The two organizations mentioned above specialize in women's health.

BEFORE YOU GO

Best Shopping: San Cristobal de las Casas
Get your wallet ready for San Cristobal de las Casas. Their market, Santo Domingo, contains everything you could ever want—artisan jewelry, leather, luggage, shoes, clothing, housewares and more. Everything is unique to the region and irresistibly adorable.

Best Surfing: Puerto Escondido
Surf, surf and more surf. The entire town is devoted to the sport, but if you're just starting out, it may be best to learn how to surf in Sayulita.

Best Street Food: Mexico City
Mexico City contains a plethora of food markets where you'll find everything from tacos to octopus and dried chiles. Street food vendors are open around the clock, so you'll always be able to find a snack that suits your cravings.

Best Architecture: Guadalajara
Check out the modern-gothic traditional Spanish homes, buildings and churches that fill the streets of Guadalajara. The architecture dates back to the 1700s and many of the buildings have been well preserved.

Best Ruins: Palenque
The ruins here are set in the jungle and were discovered in the 1950s, differentiating them from other ruins in Chichen Itza and Tulum. The Palenque ruins are peaceful and relaxed, and you're allowed entrance into several of the buildings. A walk through the back of the ruins will lead you to waterfalls and forest paradise.

Best Place to Go Out Dancing: Puerto Vallarta
For the record, Cancun almost took this award, but we prefer the relaxed vibe of Puerto Vallarta for a night out on the town. There are tons of salsa clubs and a big variety of music and people, which makes for a good time.

Best White Sand Beach: Tulum
It's just so pretty!

Iztacuattl Volcano, photo courtesy of Alasdair McLeod

MONEY & ATMS

ATMs, called *cajeros* (pronounced *caheros*) can be found throughout Mexico, while banks are limited to larger areas. All ATMs will charge you a conversion fee. On top of this, your bank at home may charge an additional fee for each transaction on your debit and credit card(s). Be sure to alert your bank(s) at home of your travel destinations and dates before you go, otherwise they may freeze your accounts for security purposes.

Some tips to help you save:

- Withdraw the maximum amount of money each time you visit an ATM. This will cut down on fees.

- Always withdraw pesos. Some ATMs offer dollars, but you will lose money in the exchange.

- If possible, avoid exchanging money at the airport. Conversion rates are notoriously more expensive in airports than in cities or towns.

- Cash is the preferred form of payment. Larger hotels, stores and restaurants usually accept credit cards, but make sure to confirm before you get the bill. Many businesses accept U.S. dollars, but you will always get the most bang for your buck using the local currency.

- Knowledge is power. Check the current rate of exchange online before you go. Do a little research of exchange houses in your area to find the best deal before you cash in.

- Keep the bulk of your money in a safe place. Only carry small amounts of cash on your person.

If you have multiple debit and/or credit cards, we recommend carrying only one with you at a time, and only when necessary. Keep the others locked up in a safe place with other important documents, like your passport.

Mexican Currency: Peso

Street Food in Mexico:
How to Eat Well and Stay Healthy

Eating on the street is the cheapest and most convenient way to eat in Mexico. Street vendors are practically everywhere selling meat, tamales, tacos, bread, sweets, fresh water of various flavors and other delicious snacks, depending where you are.

So how can you tell where is safe to eat and which stalls to avoid? Here are some tips on how to eat well on the street:

Popularity: If the stall is full of hungry locals, it's probably safe. This may seem like common sense, but at some point, you'll be tempted to skip the line and eat at the barren stall next door to save time. Don't do it! Locals know best.

Family Style: If there are women and children eating at a food stall, it's probably safe. No one is going to (knowingly) feed their child something that is harmful to digest. If a family is eating out, the food is probably delicious and well prepared.

Money Handling: You want to eat somewhere that is clean, and that includes the handling of money. Coins and bills carry a lot of germs. The person handling the money should be different from the person preparing the food; or if there is only one person at the stall, they should put a plastic bag over their hand before accepting payment. Watch for a money exchange before ordering.

Local Favorites: Try and stick to local dishes: *mole* and *tlayudas* in Oaxaca; fish, shrimp and *ceviche* along the coast; pre-hispanic cuisine in the Yucatan. Local favorites are not necessarily cheaper, but definitely more readily available and much more satisfying than say, a hotdog.

Accept Recommendations: They've never steered us wrong. Don't be shy – go ahead and ask *"donde debo comer?"* (Where should I eat?) Like we said, locals know best.

Cerveza, Guey: Glass beer bottles are recycled in Mexico, and are not thoroughly sanitized before they're refilled. Before taking a long sip from your Pacifico, Indio, Modelo or Dos Equis (just to name a few), wipe off the mouth-piece with a napkin and then run a lime along the rim. The citrus will kill the germs.

Buen Provecho!

Street food, Mexico City

CELL PHONES

It's a good idea to get a cell phone to use in Mexico, and it is a relatively inexpensive investment. You can purchase a cell phone at any OXXO (similar to 7-11) or electronics store for around 300 pesos, and add pre-paid minutes as needed.

Tip: Don't want to give up your home phone number? Most plans can be put on hold at home for around $10 a month. Call your cell phone provider for details.

To call a Mexican phone number from another country, dial:
+011-52-1 + area code + phone number.

ACCOMMODATION OPTIONS

Most budget accommodation options in Mexico are in hostels. Smaller towns will also offer vacation rentals for travelers, but unless you are planning to meet up with a group of people to split the cost, they are more expensive than renting a bed in a shared room. Hostels are a great place to meet new friends, share travel stories, and get to know the city you are in. We searched the country to find the best for your budget—the accommodation options in this guidebook are all safe, convenient, clean and staffed with friendly faces.

BARE BONES BUDGET

Mexico is a large country comprised of 31 states. A bare bones budget will fluctuate depending on when you go (low vs. high season) and where you go (large city vs. small town). To live comfortably, you'll need a daily budget of about 600 pesos. Meals on the street and in small, locally owned restaurants costs between 10–60 pesos, accommodation in hostels costs between 150–250 pesos a night, and transportation around town and between cities costs between 15–100 pesos.

Daily Budget: 600 pesos
You're Sittin' Pretty With: 1,000+ pesos

Don't forget to tip! In Mexican restaurants, 10 percent is customary. *Propinas*, or tips, for meals on the street are not expected, but spare change is appreciated.

Tip tour guides if you can afford it. Generally, you do not need to tip taxi drivers.

Tips on Bartering in Markets

Shopping? Here are some tips on how to get the best deals in Mexican markets.

- Always take a full lap around the market before you buy anything. That way you can make an informed decision on what you really want or need, and avoid impulse shopping.

- No price is fixed, and there's no harm in negotiating. Don't be shy. Asking for a lower price is common practice in open-air markets.

- Pause for a few minutes to consider the item you want to buy. The longer you wait, the more likely it is that the vendor will offer you a better deal.

- If you buy more than one item, the price should go down.

- Take a look at the quality of the item you're purchasing – how long do you think it took to hand stich that entire tapestry, blanket, or bead an entire purse? If the first price they offer seems fair for the work and time involved and you can afford it, hand over the money.

COPPER CANYON

Copper Canyon is one of the world's most beautiful canyons. Located in the state of Chihuahua, if you would like to tour this area we recommend traveling with *www.authenticcoppercanyon.com*.

MEXICAN PUBLIC HOLIDAYS

January 1: Ano Nuevo (New Year's Day)

First Monday in February: Día de la Constitucion (Constitution Day)

Third Monday in March: Natalicio de Benito Juarez (Benito Juarez's birthday)

April 5: Jueves Santo (Maundy Thursday)

April 6: Viernes Santo (Good Friday)

May 1: Día del Trabajo (Labor Day)

May 5: Cinco de Mayo

September 16: Día de la Independencia (Independence Day)

November 2: Día de los Muertos (Day of the Dead)

Third Monday of November: Día de la Revolución (Revolution Day)

December 12: Día de Guadalupe (Day of Our Lady Guadalupe)

December 25: Navidad (Christmas Day)

EMERGENCY NUMBERS

For emergencies in Mexico, dial 066, 065, 068 or 911.

066: General number for police.

065: General number for medical aid.

068: General number for fire stations.

911: A go-to emergency number used throughout most parts of Mexico.

CORDS & WIRES

Most power outlets in Mexico are the same as those found in the U.S. and Canada. To be safe, double-check that your valuable electronics run on the same voltage before you plug in.

Electrical Voltage in Mexico: 110/ 220V

WHEN TO GO

There are two distinct travel seasons in Mexico—low and high.

Low season runs from May to October and coincides with the rainy season. Hurricanes have been known to make their mark on Mexican coastlines during this period (most often between June and November) but you can score some sweet travel deals on airfare and accommodation, and the beaches are far less crowded.

High season runs from November to April, coinciding with the dry season. This is a very pleasant time to visit Mexico, as the weather is warm and less humid than in the summer months. Be advised that hotels, restaurants and airfare will be more expensive if you chose to visit during this time, especially around Christmas and the New Year.

PACKING LIST

You can purchase everything you need in Mexico, but it's always best to plan ahead!

- 3 light t-shirts
- 3 tank-tops
- 2 bathing suits/bikinis
- 1 pair of shorts
- 1 pair of jeans
- 1 pair of yoga pants/leggings
- 2 long sleeve shirts
- 1 sweatshirt/jacket
- 2 pairs of sleeping clothes
- 15-20 pairs of underwear (you can never have enough!)
- 2 bras
- 1 sports bra
- 3 dresses
- 1 long skirt
- 1 pair of sunglasses
- 1 hat
- Flip-Flops
- City flats
- Hiking boots
- Sarong
- Towel
- 1 Lock
- All necessary prescription drugs from home
- Ear plugs/Eye mask
- Pocket Spanish/English dictionary
- Flashlight
- Money belt
- One book (most hostels have a book exchange – trade yours in for another)
- Water canteen
- Watch
- Camera
- Swiss army knife

Our theory is this: If you pack smart, you can combine the above list to create dozens of outfits that work for climates in the mountains, cities and beaches.

Be sure to pack secure bikinis/bathing suits for beach activities. Sunscreen, bug spray and toiletries can be purchased in grocery stores and *tienditas* (small corner stores and markets), but it can be more difficult to find specific brands of medication and prescriptions. Talk to your doctor before you leave to either stock up on meds before you go or to get the corresponding name of your medication for refills while you are in Mexico.

Things to Leave Behind

- Excessive toiletries
- Laptop
- Expensive electronics
- Priceless/expensive jewelry
- Hairdryer/curling Iron

You can buy all the toiletries you'll need at any Mexican pharmacy, and unless you need a computer for work, we strongly recommend leaving your laptop at home. Same goes for important jewelry and expensive electronics. Theft is always a possibility when traveling through a foreign country by bus and staying in hostels, and losing something important to you can put a serious damper on your trip. Hairdryers and curling irons take up a lot of space and are unnecessary! Let go a little bit and let your hair air-dry.

TOILET PAPER

It's always a good idea to carry around toilet paper with you, as you don't know if your hostel/restaurant/bar will have it when you need it.

Note: The sewage system in Mexico can't handle toilet paper in the toilet, so you'll have to throw it in the trash can instead.

The Mexican Toilet Trick

Everybody poops, but not all Mexican toilets want to flush. This can be embarrassing, especially if you're in a public place or with a guy. How to fix this fast: if the toilet you're using won't flush, remove the toilet tank lid. Most likely, there's no water in it. Get a bucket, large bowl, or other large container, and fill it up with water from the sink. Dump the water in the toilet tank until it's full. Happy flushing!

TAMPONS

Tampons are easily found in Mexico in pharmacies, grocery stores and corner stores. Sanitary napkins are also widely available.

SMOKING IN MEXICO

Whether you're a smoker or a non-smoker, be advised that smoking in bars, clubs and restaurants is common in Mexico. If you see an ashtray, it's safe to assume you can smoke, but to be polite, ask a waiter, bartender or employee, *"puedo fumar?"* if you smoke.

"MEXICAN TIME"

You may hear people joke about "Mexican time" at points during your trip. Things move at a slower pace in Mexico than they do in other places. When you make plans with a local, don't be surprised if they show up after the scheduled time. If you're an extremely punctual person, adjusting to Mexican time may be difficult, but it can be relaxing once you get used to it—positive points include no rushing around or stressing about being late. Expect things to take longer than they would wherever you call home. This will help you avoid frustration and adjust quickly.

GETTING AROUND

Air
Domestic flights run to and from all airports in Mexico. National airlines are AeroMexico and Volaris.

Bus
Buses in Mexico are, by in large, safe and reliable. You can travel the country comfortably by bus, as long as you're willing to sacrifice a few days to get to your final destination—Mexico is huge!

Panga

Pangas are small fisherman boats that are used for day trips to islands and isolated areas along the coast. Negotiate a price with the owner before getting aboard.

Taxi

Taxis are widely available. Ask the driver how much a trip will cost before accepting the ride, if they do not use a meter. Get some information from your hostel or a local about how much a taxi ride should be to your destination, especially if you don't speak Spanish.

VISAS

Most nationalities are issued a 180-day visa upon arrival. If you would like to stay longer than 180 days, you can either apply for a work visa, which requires a Mexican business sponsor, or cross a land border and re-enter the country. Visit an embassy for help with extending visas, or other visa issues.

Make sure to check that your passport has at least six months validity before traveling and that you have blank pages for stamps and visas.

Make two copies of your passport before you leave. Leave one at home with a friend or relative, and keep another with you in a safe place in case the original is lost or stolen.

Upon entering Mexico, immigration will give you a white and green slip of paper with your date of entry. Keep it!

This is essentially your tourist visa, though it is not posted on your passport, and you will need it to exit the country. If lost, you will have to pay a fee to replace it before you will be allowed to leave Mexico.

BORDERS

Mexico is bordered by the United States to the north, and Belize and Guatemala to the south. Although you can drive from Mexico into Central America, it's much safer to fly.

Is it Safe to Cross the Border?

Yes and no. Most borders are safe, but many border towns are not. Be aware of customs regulations and rules and always be aware of your surroundings and belongings when crossing in or out of Mexico. The travel blogosphere is full of stories about corrupt officials demanding unofficial fees upon exiting Mexico. If you plan on crossing the border by land when exiting Mexico, take a bus rather than going it on your own and stay alert.

The U.S./Mexican Border

The U.S Border has sparked controversy and much debate among citizens of both countries. Barriers have been created on the United States side to prevent illegal activity and immigrants from entering the country. Despite barriers in California, Arizona and Texas, the U.S. Mexican border is considered open, or one that the public may pass through legally at any time. Those who oppose barriers between countries cite destroying animal habitats, damaging the environment and potentially compromising the health and safety of those who wish to cross the border illegally into the United States as reasons to take down barriers. Those in support of barriers along the border claim they are necessary in order to keep drugs, illegal immigrants and terrorist activity out of the United States.

The Belize Border

This border with Mexico in the south has also reportedly been used to traffic drugs, specifically cocaine, from South America into Mexico, and up to the United States. The Obama administration added Belize to its list of countries that are considered major drug producers or transit routes. We suggest flying to Belize from Mexico if possible, as reports of violence at the border have been relayed.

The Guatemalan Border

There are two main ways to cross the border from Mexico to Guatemala. One way is to pay for a shuttle ($25-30) and the other way is by public transportation ($11). The shuttle method is easy but no quicker than public transportation. They make a "breakfast" stop at an expensive roadside restaurant for almost an hour in the morning and several other unnecessary rest stops along the way. The public transportation method requires about four transfers but is surprisingly efficient. On average the trip takes about 6–8 hours depending on where you are going in Guatemala. It's best to cross during the day.

U.S. / MEXICO BORDER TOWNS

The U.S. Department of State has issued travel warnings discouraging travel to the border towns along the U.S./ Mexico border. Despite this, thousands cross the border into Mexico by land every day. We highly recommend flying into Mexico City or southern Mexico rather than crossing the border and traveling through northern Mexico.

If you're determined to cross by land, there are 32 border crossings through which you can pass. The border towns listed here are the most popular. Remember to never cross the border with weapons, and never purchase illegal narcotics in pharmacies and attempt to bring them back to the U.S.—doing so could land you up to 15 years in a Mexican prison.

Nogales

While Nogales is technically outside the scope of this book, it's such a popular destination as a border town that we can't avoid mentioning it somewhere. Indeed, for many people, Nogales serves as their very first taste of Mexico. Walking from an American city into a Mexican city in only five minutes is a trip in every sense of the word, and it serves as a vivid illustration of the numerous small differences between the two countries. Everything looks and feels different, from the architecture to the width of the streets.

Located 60 miles south of Tucson, Nogales is a small but lively city of about 212,000 people. If you're going for a day trip, we recommend parking in a safe place on the U.S. side of the border and just walking across. The McDonalds near the border is a popular place to park, and it costs $4 USD per day. Nogales is a great place to go gift-shopping: The streets are bustling with vendors and stores where you can find everything from hand-crafted chess sets to exquisitely woven baskets. It's also a great place to get your first taste of bargaining—all but unheard of in the United States, haggling with the seller for a better price is a way of life in Mexico.

As you have probably heard, you can buy pharmaceutical drugs in Nogales—and other parts of Mexico—much more cheaply than you can in the U.S. If you decide to do this, take a valid prescription with you, and make sure that it is legal to take that specific drug back into the U.S. before trying to cross the border again.

Tijuana

Tijuana sits just across from San Diego, California, at the U.S. border San Ysidro, which is reportedly one of the busiest border crossings in the world. Although Tijuana is growing into a town that's considered to be more traveler-friendly than ever, it's still also an area of much transit, home to several shantytowns of immigrants deported back from the U.S., and much poverty. Use caution when traveling through Tijuana, as this town has a reputation for crime. In recent years, drug violence has erupted throughout Tijuana, particularly in the east end of the city and through Zona Norte. Most who come through this town are merely passing through. While Tijuana has several beaches, nicer beaches are found down through Baja California, beginning in Rosarito and Ensenada.

Ciudad Juarez

Please do not cross the border into Ciudad Juarez. The area has been prone to murders in the area, specifically against women. See our Safety section for more information.

Puerto Penasco (Rocky Point)

Though it's not technically a border town (63 miles south of the border), Rocky Point is the quintessential Spring Break town, attracting so many tourists from across the border every year that it's been dubbed "Arizona's beach." With its sandy shores and beachfront resorts—not to mention its 18-year-old drinking age—it's especially popular with students. But the combination of drinking and a strange environment can be extremely volatile—have fun, but not at the cost of placing yourself in danger. Rocky Point is a relatively place to visit, but exercise caution and good judgment: avoid driving at night, stay with friends, and keep to well-lighted areas.

Our advice: Instead of going crazy, use Rocky Point as a relaxing weekend getaway. The city itself is as American-friendly as Mexican cities get; you'll find English-language menus in most of the restaurants, and many businesses even accept U.S. currency. Enjoy some delicious seafood, take in some shopping, and spend a lazy afternoon sunning on the beach. Take a good, long look at the ocean—if you're from the Southwest, this may be your best chance to see it!

— *Justyn Dillingham*

FESTIVALS IN MEXICO

Semana Santa

Semana Santa, or Holy week, runs the week of Lent, from the Friday before Palm Sunday until Easter Sunday in April. Dubbed 'Spring Break' for Mexican nationals, many people who live inland flock to the beach in search of good waves and cold *cerveza*. Parades, non-stop parties and elaborate church services are held during this time. If you're traveling during this week, especially from the city to the coast, be sure to buy your bus ticket several days in advance and call ahead for accommodation reservations.

Festival de Nuestro Senora de Guadalupe

Our lady of Guadalupe, or the Virgen de Guadalupe, is honored with a week-long festival that runs from Dec. 12—Dec. 19. She is of great importance to the people of Mexico and those who believe in her.

GET INSPIRED WITH FILMS AND BOOKS

Films:

"Y Tu Mama Tambien" (2001)

Take a road trip through Mexico with Tenoch, Julio and Ana in search of paradise on the playa. The boys learn much about life, sex and each other in this coming of age Mexican classic. Expect nudity and some heartbreak.

"Frida" (2002)

A film based on Frida Kahlo, a famous Mexican artist, starring Salma Hayek. This film chronicles the history of her personal life, many loves, art and how she became known as a Mexican icon. Frida's image is reproduced on everything from street art to interior décor throughout the country. Get to know her before you go!

"Selena" (1997)

Before Jennifer Lopez was J.Lo, she was Selena of Selena y Los Dinos, arguably the most famous Mexican-American cross-over pop artist of the 90s. Her story ends tragically, but not before she seduces Mexico into a full-on love affair with her music and persona.

"Zapatistas: Chronicle of a Rebellion" (2003)
This somewhat graphic documentary is an account of the Zapatista rebellion in Chiapas that began in 1994. The Zapatista Army of National Liberation held a rebellion against the federal government of Mexico, fighting for equal human rights of the indigenous population of Mexico.

Books

"*Don Quixote*" by Miguel de Cervantes
"*The Lacuna*" by Barbara Kingsolver

For More Info, Check Out These Awesome Mexico-Inspired Travel Blogs

www.gomexicoguide.com
www.marginalboundaries.com

Virgen de Guadalupe

The Virgen de Guadalupe is considered the mother of Latin America and Mexico. After the Spanish conquered the indigenous population of Mexico in 1519, the locals found it very difficult to convert to Catholicism because they believed in the elements—sun, Earth, moon, rain. After the image of the Virgen de Guadalupe appeared, the people felt like they fit into this new religion because they could see themselves in her, and converted to Catholicism. Her image is considered sacred and her church, the second most-visited religious site in the world, is built in the original place where she first appeared and can still be visited today.

NO TE PUEDO VER
PERO MI ACORDEON
LE CANTA A TU CORAZON
GRACIAS

I CAN´T SEE YOU BUT
ANYTIME I STRUM A KEY
I CAN HEAR YOUR HEART BEAT
THANKS A LOT

CULTURE & CUSTOMS

CULTURE AND CUSTOMS

As a foreigner, or *extranjera*, no one expects you to know the ins and outs of Mexican culture, but it is important to have some background knowledge on Mexican customs. Showing respect to locals will go a long way, as will attempting to speak a little Spanish.

In general, Mexicans are a warm and vibrant people, who value family and religion, as well as an enjoyment of life. Things move at a slower pace in Mexico than in other cultures, so it's important to come with a little patience and an open mind.

HISTORY

Spanish armies conquered indigenous Mexico during the period of 1519 – 1521, but before they arrived, highly developed cultures of several different indigenous populations ruled, worked and thrived in cities, towns and tribes throughout Mexico. The Spanish brought Catholicism and European culture to those they conquered, and deemed many indigenous religious and cultural practices barbaric and uncivilized. Temples, long established government buildings, social and economic systems and methods of trade were destroyed and turned into Catholic cathedrals and Spanish government palaces, and a dramatically different way of life emerged. Cortes' Spanish colony ruled Mexico for almost 300 years, and the blend of the Spanish and indigenous created the mestizo population of modern Mexico.

Independence from Spain was claimed on Sept. 16, 1810, after almost 10 years of war. A republic was established in 1824. In the early 1900's, a revolution occurred due to economic and social problems, resulting in the 1917 constitution, which is still in place today.

The rich history of Mexico is apparent all over the country, but especially in Mexico City's Zocalo. Take a trip to the newly discovered Aztec ruins, step inside the Catholic cathedral and get a glimpse of modern buildings that surround the square for a clear picture of the blend of pre-Hispanic, Spanish and modern cultural influences that make up today's Mexico.

FAMILY AND RELIGION

Family and religion are at the central hub of Mexican society and culture. Avoid any derogatory statements about these topics, as they could get you into trouble, or at the very least, a fiery debate. Most people in Mexico identify as Catholics or Christians and belong to a close knit, large family. In the 2000 census, 75 percent of Mexico's population identified themselves as Roman Catholic.

With such a strong religious background, abortion is a topic of conversation to avoid, as it is illegal and controversial in most areas of the country, with the exception of Mexico City. While you are free to make your own decisions, it's important to be aware of the culture you are immersed in, and as a visitor, show respect for its customs and beliefs.

La Virgen de Guadalupe is a saint and considered the holy mother of Mexico. Defacing her image is like burning the Mexican flag. Many believe she is a protector of those who believe in her.

GREETING

It's important to say hello to those you meet, usually with a handshake, or a single kiss on a cheek. Exchanging greetings to people you come in contact with is extremely important, and is a way to show respect. It is considered rude to not say hello, especially in small towns where often, everyone knows each other. To break into local culture, smile and say hello.

Some common phrases:

- *Hola, como estas?* Hello, how are you.
- *Buenos dias.* Good morning.
- *Buenos tardes.* Good afternoon.
- *Buenas noches.* Good night.
- *Que tal?* What's up?

INDIGENOUS CULTURE

Representing about 13 percent of the country, or roughly 12 million people, Mexico has one of the largest indigenous populations in Latin America. Many still speak native languages, practice and preserve native customs, and work in the agricultural industry. Ruins from the Aztecs and Mayas are large tourist attractions. Indigenous markets may be found throughout the country, though most indigenous people reside in the southern and central states of Oaxaca, Chiapas, Veracruz, Puebla, Yucatan, Guerrero, Hidalgo and Mexico City. Their textiles, handcrafts, jewelry and art are exquisite, and very unique to the region.

Several organizations help support indigenous populations preserve their culture and customs. Find out more about volunteering in our Volunteer section on page 201.

MACHISMO CULTURE
AND HOW IT AFFECTS YOU

Latin America is famous for its *machismo* culture—meaning, men are considered to be the dominant sex. It's something you'll encounter from time to time, in conversations and on the road, but it shouldn't affect your trip that much unless you date a Mexican man. Women tend to live with their families until they get married, and many women marry and have children at a young age. Even though Mexico has come a long way in terms of women's rights, a single woman living on her own is not always the norm. Don't be surprised if you hear a man call out a term of endearment, get a door held open for you, or offers for a travel companion. Remember that a polite, but direct, *no, thank you*, is always in your realm of possibility.

People may give you strange looks if you say you're traveling alone and ask if you're married or have a boyfriend. If you don't want to answer this, say you're meeting up with friends, and your boyfriend is coming too, even if you don't have one. This little white lie could help you avoid a potentially awkward conversation.

DEALING WITH CATCALLS

From time to time you will encounter catcalling—when men call out, or "holler" at you and tell you how beautiful you are, for example. It can be annoying, but it's usually harmless. Try not to take offense. If you are walking and are getting catcalled, walk forward with purpose and ignore the comments. Responding or acknowledging catcalls can sometimes encourage the situation and make things more uncomfortable.

CURRENT POLITICS

Today's modern Mexican government is similar in structure to the United States with core, dominant political parties, open elections and executive, legislative and judicial branches. Presidents hold office for six years and may not run for a second term. The most recent national election took place in July 2012, in which voters selected a new President, Senate and Chamber of Deputies. There are 31 states in Mexico, with a population of approximately 13 million people. The election of 2000 was the first election since the Mexican Revolution that the opposition defeated the party in government. In recent years, youth have begun to take an interest in Mexican politics, rallying and marching in demonstrations in the capital, demanding fair coverage and access to information on elections, presidential candidates and upcoming legislation that will affect the greater population.

POLICE

It's unfortunate, but Mexican police are not always on your side. Incidents of corruption have been reported, and while some members of the police are honest, others are looking to take advantage of bribes in any way they can. The best way to deal with them is to fly under their radar – don't buy or do drugs, pee in public, or go on the beaches at night. If for some reason you do have a run in with a member of the Mexican police force, comply with their requests.

Some things to know:

- By law, male police officers can only search male civilians. In order for your body to be searched, it must be done by a female officer.

- The Mexican police force is divided into three entities: federal, state and municipal, or *federal, estado y municipal*. Military officers are the highest-ranking officers in the country, and are usually wearing protective facial masks and all-black clothing.

- Corruption within local police is rampant, and many officers solicit bribes. If you get stuck and are asked for money, comply.

DRUGS AND NARCO TRAFFICKING

It's no secret Mexico is currently in the midst of what the media has dubbed the "drug war."

Narcos and drug trafficking are heavily prevalent in northern parts of Mexico, close to the United States border, as well as other areas throughout the country, and have claimed domination of Mexico's black market.

Gangs, narcos, and/or drug traffickers target rival Mexicans who are considered competition, or who don't comply with their rules. For this reason, it is highly unlikely that visitors or tourists should encounter them, especially if you stay away from drugs and other illegal activity.

While much of Mexico is a beautiful, warm and friendly place, it's an unfortunate truth that this war has contributed to an increase in drug-related deaths since 2006. According to the U.S. Department of State, most casualties have been directly involved in narcotic trafficking. Out of about 34,000 deaths, only 111, or .003 percent, have been U.S. and foreign citizens.

There is one giant way you can ensure your safety from narcos and drug traffickers while in Mexico: don't buy or do drugs!

Not only do they lower your inhibitions and your ability to stay safe, but as a tourist, when you buy drugs in Mexico, you are contributing to the underground narcotic trade that is responsible for thousands of deaths a year. You can best protect yourself by staying away from drugs (yes, even marijuana) when traveling.

DID YOU KNOW?

1. Mexico is the largest Spanish speaking country in the world, and the second most populated country in Latin America, next to Brazil.

2. 80% of Mexico's exports went to the United States in 2010.

3. Carlos Slim Helu, the owner and operator of Mexico's Telcel, is *Forbes Magazine*'s richest man in the world.

4. Peyote, a hallucinogenic cactus, is still used by indigenous groups in religious ceremonies, and grows throughout the country.

5. Mexicans believe that on Día De Los Muertos, deceased loved ones are allowed to return to the mortal world to visit friends and relatives. Graves are decorated with candles to help guide the spirits home.

MEXICO CITY

Mexico City is massive and can be overwhelming for a first time visitor, especially if you've never been to a major Latin American capital. There are millions of people, bustling streets, metro lines stuffed to the brim, countless markets, distinct neighborhoods and literally hundreds of museums. Walking streets that surround downtown are bursting at the seams with people while street performers work hard for tips. Thick layers of culture and social status are piled on top of each other; layers that can easily be distinguished by taking a trip to the Zocalo to see pre-Hispanic ruins. If you take a few minutes to watch the people around you, you'll see high class businessmen in shiny shoes and expensive suits on their way to a meeting; young mothers holding babies; street vendors selling everything from perfume to a cleansing of the mind, body and spirit; tattooed youth smoking cigarettes to pass the time, and fellow travelers snapping photos of it all.

As they say in Mexico, de todo un poco.

The best way to see Mexico City is deciding first what it is that draws you here – is it the culture? History? Food? Art? Architecture? Nightlife? Sheer size of it all? Pick a few focal points, choose a reasonable number of museums and places of interest that you can get to on your own, and then book tours to see the rest. It would take years to see the whole city in its entirety, and doing everything should not be the ultimate goal. Over-extending yourself and packing your days full of plans will only cause stress and put a damper on your D.F. experience. Be realistic, go with the flow, and pack some patience in that day bag you're clutching close to your body. The people are lively, the food is delicious, and there are endless possibilities to entertain yourself; use some common sense and you'll blend right in.

Best Museum:
Anthropology Museum

Best Ruins:
The pyramids at Teotihuacan

Best Neighborhood for Nightlife:
La Condesa

HOW TO GET THERE

Mexico City's international airport is the country's main travel hub, with domestic and international flights arriving daily from around the world. Since it is such a large airport, flights that land in Mexico City tend to be less expensive than those that go to more remote areas of the country. When you arrive, purchase a ticket for an authorized taxi from the stand inside the terminal; it should be near the exit. Rates are fixed. Once outside, wait in line for a taxi. Give the driver your ticket and destination information.

Airport Code: MEX

There are four main bus stations in Mexico. You will probably use the TAPO bus station most often, but just in case, here is information on all four:

Terminal Central Norte
Buses depart here to Northern Mexico and the U.S., plus a few other places, including Chiapas, Guanajuato, Jalisco, Michoacan and Veracruz. Metro Stop: Autobuses del Norte

Terminal Centro Sur
Buses depart here to Southern Mexico, including Chiapas, Guerrero, Puebla, Oaxaca, Tabasco and Veracruz. Metro Stop: Tasquena

Terminal de Oriente TAPO

Buses depart here to the south and east, including Campeche, Chiapas, Puebla, Oaxaca, Quintana Roo, Tlaxcala, Tabasco, Veracruz and the Yucatan. Metro Stop: San Lazaro

Terminal Centro Poniente

These buses head west, including Guerrero, Jalisco, Michoacan, Nayarit, Queretaro, State of Mexico, Sinaloa and Sonora. Metro Stop: Observatorio

Before you leave Mexico City by bus, check online for departure information. First class bus websites list which station specific buses leave from. You can either take the metro or a taxi to the bus station. Plan to arrive at least 20 minutes before the scheduled departure time to ensure you have enough time to buy a ticket. We recommend taking a taxi, especially if you're traveling with valuables, but the choice is yours.

Mexican Bus Lines:

ETN: www.etn.com.mx

Estrella de Oro: www.estrelladeoro.com.mx

Omnibuses de Mexico: www.odm.com.mx

ADO: www.ado.com.mx

MEXICO CITY

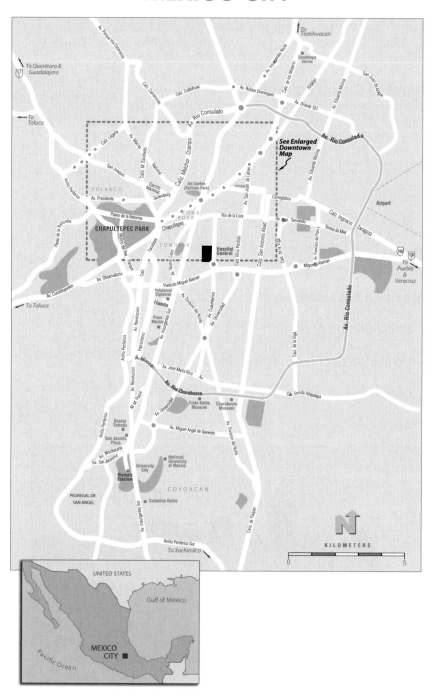

MEXICO CITY DOWNTOWN AREA

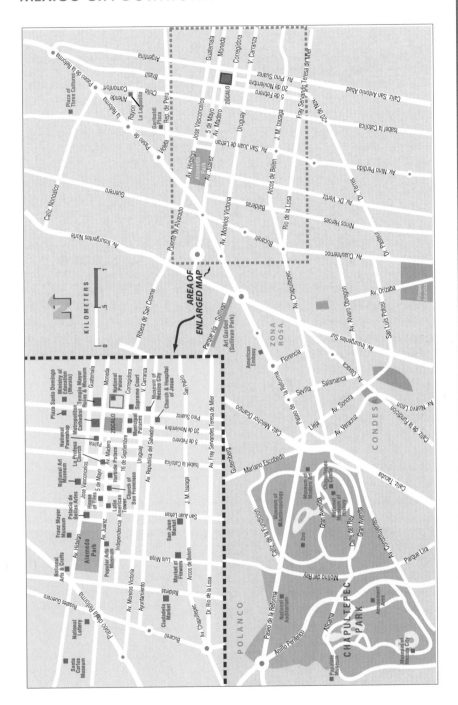

MEXICO CITY METRO SYSTEM

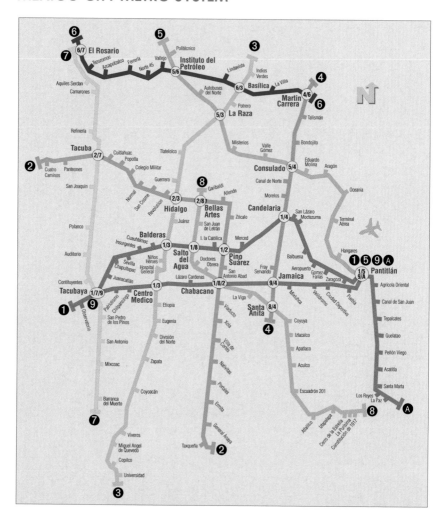

THINGS TO KNOW

Much of the Safety section in this book deals with tips that apply to Mexico City. Read it again to refresh your memory about staying alert and walking with purpose, how to avoid common scams and stay safe in the capital.

It's crowded almost everywhere, all the time. The amount of traffic can be daunting. If you have to be somewhere at a specific time, like the bus station, give yourself 15 extra minutes than you think you'll need to get to your destination.

- La Zona Rosa is the unofficial gay neighborhood of Mexico City, and is easily distinguished by the amount of sex shops and same-sex innuendos on signs, club fronts and couples displaying affection in public.

- La Condesa is an upscale neighborhood with beautiful apartments, houses and parks. It's a nice place to people watch and visit for a softer side of the big city. It's safe and posh, and is a great neighborhood to go out in at night.

- The Zocalo is where you'll find the most museums per block in the entire city. Many hostels are located in and around the plaza, and it's a big tourist destination. For this reason, hostels in this area of the city may get infiltrated with street noise at night; bring earplugs.

- Every year, people from all over Mexico flock to the capital in search of opportunities, work, or to attend university. There is a wide range of the social classes, as there is in any capital city. You'll encounter many types of people from all over the country and the world. Remember that most Mexicans are polite by nature, so do your best to show the same courtesy, no matter who you're speaking to.

- Café El Popular is located adjacent to the Zocalo, and is open 24 hours. They offer cheap, local fare and are famous for their coffee and pastries.

- Elevation in Mexico City is above 7,300 feet. If you're coming from a very low elevation, be sure to drink a lot of water and take it easy for the first few days of your trip to avoid altitude sickness.

- We recommend staying around the Zocalo for easy access to the main sites and points of interest. There are several metro stops in the area, and it's easy to get to and from.

Cabs

If you catch a cab off the street, the license plate should match the number on the permit posted in the window. There should also be a photo of the driver. If you're not sure about where you're going, you can always ask your hostel staff to call you a secure taxi to pick you up. This service is especially helpful if you don't speak Spanish. Rates are fixed and more expensive than catching a cab off the street, but secure cabs are safer.

Buses

We do not recommend taking buses around Mexico City. They are confusing and hard to navigate. Stick to cabs, the metro, and walking.

Metro

Keep your wits about you on the metro. It's 3 pesos for a single ride, and cars are packed to the brim at all hours of the day. Keep your purse or bag zipped shut and held close to your body when in crowded areas, and if you can, try to stand by the door. Cars can be hard to exit, and if you're not the pushy type, you'll miss your stop. The system is set up like almost all major metros around the world – buy a ticket at the *taquilla* (buy more than one ticket at a time if you'll be using the metro often – lines are long), enter the station, and follow signs for the direction your headed. If you can, don't pull out a map in the station, as this will draw attention to you and signal that you're distracted, and/or lost. Instead, find the metro map that is posted on the wall – there is at least one at every stop.

THINGS TO DO

Teotihuacan

Visit the pyramids and ruins at Teotihuacan, located on the outskirts of Mexico City. Visitors are welcome to climb pyramids. We recommend taking a guided tour, since we heard that buses traveling to Teotihuacan are often held up on the highway. Bring water, your camera, a hat and sunscreen.

Templo de Nuestro Senora de Guadalupe
This is the second most-visited religious site in the world, with more than 2 million visitors a year. The original image of the Virgen de Guadalupe can be viewed inside the church. Those who visit often bring an offering to the Virgen; most often candles or flowers. The most crowded day at the temple is December 12, which is considered the Virgen's birthday. Last year over 5 million people came to honor her.

Zocalo and Surrounding Sites
Take a walk around the Zocalo to see the largest cathedral on the continent, ruins and museum next door, government palace and street performers. Around the Zocalo are several other points of interest, including the Palacio de las Bellas Artes and the Templo Mayor.

Frida Kahlo and Diego Rivera Museum
Visit the house where Frida Kahlo grew up and later shared with her husband, Diego Rivera. It's also known as 'the blue house,' or 'casa azul.' Inside are collections of Frida and Diego's art, collections of their journals, and her preserved bedroom and a collection of personal items. There is also a gift shop downstairs.

Chapultepec Park and Museums
This massive park holds multiple museums. If you have to choose one, head to the Anthropology Museum. Make sure you have a few hours to spend inside the museum – it's huge and covers the history of all of Mexico's pre-Hispanic civilizations up to the present day, with art, architecture, pottery, maps, jewelry, cultural and historical information on groups such as the Aztecs, Mayans, Toltecs and various other cultures from all over Mexico.

Lucha Libre Wrestling
You'll want to go with a group, but a lucha libre wrestling match is one of the most unique things you can do while you're in Mexico City. Wrestlers wear masks and go to extremes to please and shock crowds.

Xochimilco
This is a UNESCO World Heritage Site, and is located on the southern edge of Mexico City. It is a network of canals and artificial islands that date back to Aztec times, and include a floating garden. You can rent a ride around on canals for an hour or more, which includes a stop to an artisan market. Don't forget your camera!

Teotihuacan pyramid

ACCOMMODATION

Mundo Joven Youth Hostel
This large hostel is located right on the Zocalo, and has a rooftop bar, laundry services, shared and private rooms, Wi-Fi, a restaurant, free breakfast, shared kitchen, a tour desk, 24-hour reception, security, bilingual staff and free walking tours of the city. Rooms are basic and clean. Even though the hostel is large compared

to other accommodation options in the city, it's usually full of people, and staff makes a great attempt at offering group activities and providing a social environment without feeling overwhelming.

Cost: 180 pesos for a bed in a shared dorm

The easiest way to direct a taxi driver to Mundo Joven Hostel is to ask them to head to the cathedral in the Zocalo. If you're facing the cathedral, the hostel is behind it towards your left hand side on Guatemala Street.

Republica de Guatemala 4
Colonia Centro Historico,
Mexico City
555-518-1726
info@mundojovenhostels.com
www.mundojovenhostels.com

Hostel Amigo

This smaller hostel offers almost all of the same amenities as Mundo Joven, and is in the same neighborhood. A travel agency is stationed in the hostel, which makes buying bus tickets, plane tickets and booking tours easy and convenient. Staff is bi-lingual, free breakfast, comfortable common areas, shared kitchen, funky décor, bar inside for mingling, 24-hour security and shared bathrooms. Rooms are basic and clean.

Cost: 190 pesos for a bed in a shared dorm

Isabel La Catolica 61
Colonia Centro Historico,
Mexico City
555-512-3464
info@hostelamigo.com
www.hostelamigo.com

SHOPPING

There is great shopping in Mexico City. There are street vendors set up throughout the main Zocalo square, and tons of markets with handmade goods.

BAJA SUR

The southern coast of Baja California has a dual personality. It's both flashy and touristy in places like Cabo San Lucas, and quiet and laid-back in areas like nearby La Paz. It's the kind of place people come to fish and party; maybe take a booze cruise or two. In Cabo San Lucas, the up-all-night-life is very popular with Spring breakers, while La Paz caters to an older crowd, looking to golf, sail and deep sea fish. Swim with whale sharks on either tip of the peninsula, float past a few seals, snap some photos of exotic birds while sipping on a *cerveza* or fruity cocktail – Baja Sur is beautiful.

Baja California Sur

Best Place to Swim with Whale Sharks:
La Paz

Best Place Off the Beaten Path:
Todos Santos

Best Way to Ensure A Hangover:
Drink free drinks at ladies night in Cabo!

CABO SAN LUCAS

Welcome to Los Cabos, where cash is king. The backpacker scene here is somewhat lacking, and to be completely honest, Cabo is not the place to go if you're on a serious budget. There are no hostels and it's somewhat isolated from the rest of Mexico, located on the Baja peninsula. The beaches are beautiful, the weather is hot, and spring break draws many tourists looking to party throughout the months of March and April. If you're looking to explore mainland Mexico and don't have a lot of time and/or money, we'd recommend saving Cabo for your next trip.

That's not to say that there aren't things to do here – the fishing community is huge, and on a good day, you can catch marlin, mahi mahi and tuna. The diving is great, especially at Cabo Pulmo, a diverse coral reef and protected area about 60 miles north of Cabo. Snorkel with tropical fish, party till you drop, eat delicious seafood and the local *machaca*, and if you come during the season, you can swim with whale sharks. If you're interested in getting off the beaten path, there are mountainous communities that welcome tourists and less-touristy La Paz is just a few hours away.

HOW TO GET THERE

Airport
Los Cabos international airport is about a 30-minute drive from Cabo San Lucas by taxi, but it's much cheaper to take a shuttle. Flights arrive daily from domestic and international airports. You can also fly into La Paz, which is about an hour and a half drive by car, three hours by bus.

Airport code: SJD.

Getting to and from the airport is easy, as long as you're willing to pay for a shuttle. Taxis can cost anywhere from 600–700 pesos. The cheapest shuttle company we found was CAPE Travel: *www.cape-travel.com*.

Bus
Cabo's main bus station is small and easy to miss. To get there, take a local city bus heading away from the beach with 'Soriana' marked on the front window (Soriana is a large grocery store). The bus station is across from the Pemex station. Make sure to ask your bus driver to let you know when to get off.

You probably won't have to take a city bus while you're in Cabo, as most things are within walking distance, but you may want to hop on a water taxi to get to some of the other beaches in the area that are the best for snorkeling. For the best deal, negotiate directly with the captain instead of representatives who walk up and down the marina looking to sell rides.

- Cabo is nestled on the southern point of Baja California. The Mar de Cortez is great for swimming, but the Pacific Ocean side has dangerous rip tides – use extreme caution if swimming in the Pacific! The best beach for swimming is Playa Medano.

- As a general rule of thumb, stay off the beaches at night, no matter where you are.

- The local city bus costs 9.5 pesos.

- Clubs are located throughout downtown, and nightlife is huge. El Squid Row is arguably the most famous.

- Lots of goods and services are priced in dollars, so having a little USD isn't necessarily a bad thing. However, if what you're looking to purchase is priced in pesos, you'll get a better deal paying in the local currency.

- Eat seafood while you're here. It's fresh, usually caught the morning of preparation, and delicious. Some local dishes are ceviche, fish tacos and shrimp any way you like them.

THINGS TO DO

El Arco
Take a water taxi to El Arco for a day in the sun. The arch itself is beautiful, and colonies of sea lions are usually lounging at its base. Beaches in this area are Lovers Beach and Divorce Beach – funny names, but both are great places to soak up the sun for an afternoon. Some of the best snorkeling can be done here. Rent equipment from your boat driver.

Whale Watch
Whale watch along Baja's peninsula. Whales migrate here from November through March, and we heard they can even be spotted from the beach during this time! Looking for more adventure? Dive with whale sharks from November through February. Sunshine Dive Company comes highly recommended.

www.divecabo.com

Play in the Water
Fish for marlin, mahi mahi, tuna and shrimp. Ask a restaurant to throw your catch on the grill for a delicious meal. You can also take a stand-up paddle board lesson, rent jet skis, parasail, kayak or swim on Medano beach.

Cabo Pulmo
Visit Cabo Pulmo, a diverse marine reserve and coral reef, to see wildlife in this national protected area, located about 60 miles north of Cabo San Lucas. Plans have been made to develop this delicate area into a massive tourist destination, with hotels, resorts, golf courses and an airport, so visit while you can!

www.cabopulmovivo.org

Feel like getting away for a few days? Todos Santos and La Paz are just a few hours away by bus.

Hotel Olas

Clean, comfortable and safe, this is our pick for the best budget hotel in Cabo. Located on a quiet street about four blocks from the beach and walking distance from all things downtown, the location is ideal, and the front desk staff is very friendly and helpful. Breakfast not included, but there are small restaurants close by, Wi-Fi, air conditioning and 24-hour reception.

Cost: 400 pesos for a private room

Revolucion and Gomez Farias
Centro, Cabo San Lucas
624-143-1780
hotelolas_csl@hotmail.com

Cabo Inn

This hotel's amenities are great – small rooftop pool and lounge area complete with palapas and shaded reading area, shared kitchen, Wi-Fi, hot water and comfortable beds – but reservations are not flexible. The bilingual staff can provide airport transportation if booked far enough in advance, and help you book tours.

Cost: 560–600 pesos for a private room with one person; 845–900 pesos for a private room with 2 people.

20 de Noviembre y Leona Vicario

Centro, Cabo San Lucas
US Phone: 619-819-2727
International Phone:
624-143-0819
info@caboinnhotel.com
www.caboinnhotel.com

Norman Diego's The Mexican Inn

This bed and breakfast wins the best décor award. Each room is named after a famous Mexican woman, and rooms are decorated accordingly. There's a beautiful central courtyard with a fountain and flowers. Bathrooms are equally impressive, with colored tile and spacious showers. It's in downtown, within walking distance of the

marina, beach and nightlife. If you're looking to splurge but not break the bank, stay at the Mexican Inn.

Cost: 600 pesos for a private room.

Abasolo and September 16 Centro, Cabo San Lucas 624-143-4987 themexicaninn@hotmail.com www.themexicaninn.com

························ ## SHOPPING ························

Shopping in Cabo is pretty standard. There are several stores and an outdoor market along the marina, a Liverpool mall downtown, and boutiques along practically every street. If you're looking to buy gifts or souvenirs and plan to visit other places in Mexico, we recommend you save your money and space in your backpack for larger, less touristy cities where things are less expensive.

LA PAZ

Located on the eastern side of the southern coast of Baja California, La Paz is a small beach city full of retired ex-patriots and Mexican families. It's different from Cabo San Lucas in that it's not a major spring break destination, meaning La Paz is light on the late night clubs and all-inclusive, high-rise resorts. Most people who come to La Paz come specifically to relax, fish and golf. The best beaches are located north of the city and, for the most part, are quiet. Funky art galleries can be stumbled upon throughout the city, but most activities here are centered around the ocean, and almost all of them require a guide or company to provide transportation and equipment.

La Paz and Cabo San Lucas are fairly isolated from mainland Mexico in that they're situated on the Baja peninsula, and can be expensive to get to and from. La Paz is also not the cheapest place in terms of accommodation – there are no hostels here, just a few budget hotels. Unless you're looking for a quiet beach town in Baja California to relax on for a few days, skip this beach community, especially if you're short on time or money and want to visit other places in mainland Mexico.

HOW TO GET THERE

If you're headed to La Paz from mainland Mexico, you have a few options: you can fly to the city's international airport, and take a taxi, shuttle, or bus into town, or you can make your way to Mazatlan and ride the Baja Ferry to La Paz overnight. The trip via ferry can be pricey, especially if you want a room with a bed to sleep in, and takes about 15 hours. Visit *www.bajaferries.com* for more information.

Coming from Cabo San Lucas, you can take a local Aguila bus to La Paz for around 200 pesos or less. Buses leave several times a day, and the ride takes about three hours. You will get dropped off on the *malecon* in La Paz, directly in front of the ocean. For bus schedules, go to *www.peninsulaejecutivo.com*.

La Paz International Airport Code: LAP

THINGS TO KNOW

La Paz is a fairly quiet town when it comes to nightlife. Your best bet is to head to the *malecón* for dinner and drinks with an ocean view to watch the sunset. Some restaurants and bars have live music and dancing. Ask around for recommendations, or just follow your ears.

You may notice that there is not much room to lay out on the beach along the malecón. The best beaches are north of La Paz, and are usually quiet, especially on weekdays. Spacious beaches start at the north end of the malecón, and continue on for 15 miles. Playa Tecolote and Playa Balandra are popular.

- There's a wide variety of international cuisine, but the freshest food in La Paz is always the local catch of the day.

- There are no hostels in La Paz, and when we were there, we also didn't see many tourists. There are some reasonably priced hotels, and while they're safe and clean (for the most part), none that we found have a very social atmosphere.

- Carnival is the biggest festival of the year in La Paz, and accommodations fill up quickly during this week. Book in advance if you plan to visit during carnival.

For more information, visit *www.allaboutlapaz.net*, or *www.vivalapaz.com*.

THINGS TO DO

Anthropology Museum
The Anthropology Museum of La Paz is a very informative museum about the history of the city and surrounding region of Baja California. It contains fossils, artifacts, art and information on the conquest of La Paz by Hernan Cortez, but be advised that this information is not posted in English, so if you don't speak Spanish, you'll be hard pressed to read captions and descriptions of things on display. Cost is 35 pesos to enter, and an extra 45 pesos for the use of a camera.

Espiritu Santos Island
This small island off the coast of La Paz is a UNESCO World Heritage

Site, and is home to coral reefs, hundreds of types of fish and other marine life. It is a great place to snorkel and spend a day. If you're lucky, you can also see dolphins and whales from the beach.

Beach Activities
Swimming, snorkeling, diving, stand up paddle boarding, kayaking and sailing are all possible along any of the six beaches to the north of La Paz. Equipment can be rented at the beach of your choice. Many tour operators set up on the sand for easy access. For specific tour operator contact information, visit *www.allaboutlapaz.net*.

Swim with Whale Sharks
The best time to swim with these massive, but harmless animals is from December through March. Be sure to ask your tour operator if they're around La Paz when you choose to go.

Fish
Deep sea spear fishing and sport fishing trips are a major draw for La Paz. People come from all over the world to fish for marlin, tuna, yellowtail and grouper, just to name a few.

Todos Santos Day Trip
You can also take a day trip to the nearby mining town of Todos Santos, which we heard is a funky town full of character and charm. You can chose to go with a tour operator, or take the bus on your own. Todos Santos is about an hour and a half from La Paz.

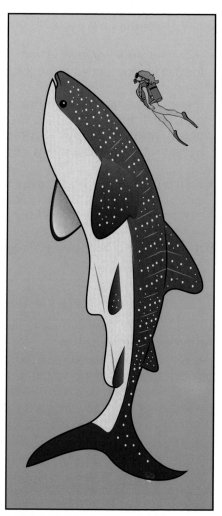

Whale Shark

ACCOMMODATION

Pension California

This small hotel is within walking distance of the bus terminal and *malecon*, and while it's not the most pristine place we've ever stayed, it offers a quiet place to sleep for your visit to La Paz. 24-hour reception, Wi-Fi, shared outdoor kitchen, hot water, spacious outdoor common areas, colorful décor and art. Note that a few families call this hotel home, at least for the time being, but it is also popular with backpackers and is a decent budget option. Staff is friendly and helpful, but note that not all are bilingual.

Cost: 280 pesos for a private room

Avenida Degollado 209
Colonia Centro
La Paz
612-122-2896
pensioncalifornia@prodigy.net.mx
facebook.com/pensioncalifornia

Hotel Arte Museo Yeneka

We didn't realize this place was a hotel until we stepped inside to admire the funky art gallery at the front of the building. This quirky hotel offers a free shot of tequila with check in, hot water, breakfast, a shared kitchen and clean private rooms. Décor is a mix of interesting and peculiar – you'll know the place by the life-size horse made of palm trees stationed out front.

Cost: 380 pesos a night for a private room

Fco. Madero 1520
Colonia Centro
La Paz
612-125-4688
hotelyeneka@hotmail.com
facebook.com/yenekahotel

SHOPPING

La Paz is full of art galleries and small artisan shops, but isn't really the place you want to go to shop. Nearby Cabo San Lucas has more shopping opportunities, though it's geared largely towards travelers.

PACIFIC COAST

The Pacific Coast is full of laid-back beach communities with big personalities. Our favorite is Sayulita, but visitors enjoy Puerto Vallarta and Mazatlan as well, especially from November through April when the weather is warm and the beaches are full. Learn to surf, paddle board or dive, eat well and be merry. *Orale, guey.*

─── TOP ⭐ PICKS ───

Best Place to Learn How to Surf:
Sayulita

Best Day Trip: Yelapa

Best Hangover Cure: Cielo Rojo

MAZATLAN

Stretched along six miles of sunny beaches, Mazatlan, dubbed the "Pearl of the Pacific," offers more than just a good time for spring breakers. With multiple beaches, street art, an active ex-pat community and a rich historical center, not to mention the second tallest natural lighthouse in the world, there's plenty to see and do here.

STATE OF SINALOA

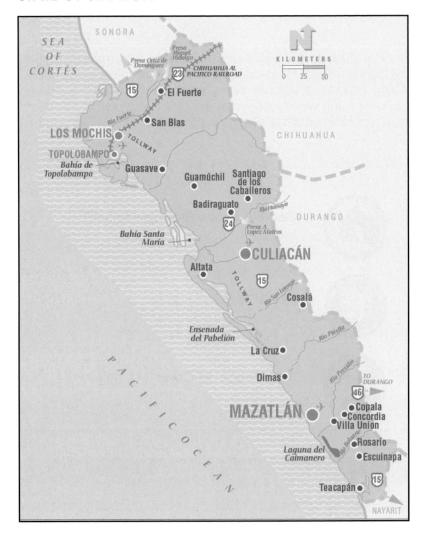

NUEVO MAZATLAN & EMERALD BAY

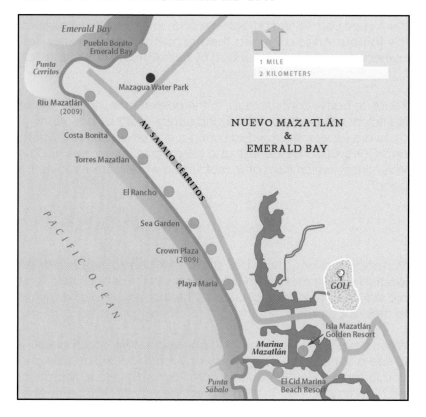

1 MILE
2 KILOMETERS

NUEVO MAZATLÁN
&
EMERALD BAY

Emerald Bay
Pueblo Bonito
Emerald Bay
Punta
Cerritos
Mazagua Water Park
Riu Mazatlán
(2009)
AV SABALO CERRITOS
Costa Bonita
Torres Mazatlán
El Rancho
PACIFIC OCEAN
Sea Garden
Crown Plaza
(2009)
Playa Maria
GOLF
Isla Mazatlán
Golden Resort
Marina
Mazatlán
Punta
Sábala
El Cid Marina
Beach Resort

If you're into water sports, you'll love Mazatlan. Visitors can kayak, parasail, sport fish, surf, or hop on a boat in any of the city's seven beaches. Walk along the malecón, or boardwalk, for one of the most spectacular sunsets Mexico has to offer, or just lounge in the sun – the average temperature year round is about 82 degrees.

Mazatlan also offers a rich historical center in El Centro, or downtown. Here you will find art galleries and an architecture museum, the famous Angela Peralta theatre, central open-air market, cathedral and plazas surrounded by cobblestone streets, sidewalk cafes and neighborhood shops.

Ready to party? *Zona Dorada*, or the golden zone, houses tons of nightclubs where you can drink and dance until the early morning. Clubs are especially crowded during spring break, Semana Santa and Carnival, so be careful and be aware! The largest disco is Valentino's, which from afar, looks like a white castle above the beach.

HOW TO GET THERE

Mazatlan has one main bus station, or *centro de camiones*, located a few blocks from the beach, and taxis and *pulmonias* are stationed outside at all hours of the day, ready to drive visitors to their accommodation.

When traveling to Mazatlan, and anywhere in Mexico, make sure to ride a first class bus line – you'll pay more, but will be safe and comfortable. If you're heading from Puerto Vallarta to Mazatlan, we recommend TAP. The 9-hour bus ride will cost 400 pesos one-way, and they give you snacks! You can find bus schedules at *www.tap.com.mx*.

The General Rafael Buelna International Airport has international, domestic and charter flights. Flying domestically within Mexico will save time, but hurt your wallet. We recommend taking buses whenever possible.

THINGS TO KNOW

• Mazatlan does not have a wide selection of youth hostels, but budget hotels can be found throughout the city. Expect to pay between 250–400 pesos for a room. Many hotels will offer a deal if you stay for three days or more.

- Nearly 1 million tourists visit Mazatlan each year, and it's easily navigated for English-speaking foreigners.

- Pick up a *Pacific Pearl*, the local English newspaper, for up-coming events, local information and a map of the city. *www.pacificpearl.com*

- *Pulmonias* are a kind of open air taxis that are specific to Mazatlan, and in general, they're more expensive than regular taxis.

- Always negotiate a price with your taxi or pulmonia driver before accepting a ride. If you cannot come to an agreement, simply walk away and wait for the next driver. This practice is standard in Mazatlan.

- Pulmonias can be rented for a half or full day, and are a great way to get around town. Expect to pay between 200–350 pesos. Half day should be around 200, full day between 300–350. It also depends on the driver and how good your negotiating skills are.

Pulmonia

- It can get cold in the winter. Bring a sweater and wear pants if you plan to explore the city after the sun goes down.

- Behind Rio de Janeiro and New Orleans, Mazatlan hosts the third largest Carnival celebration in the world. If you plan to visit Mazatlan the third week in February, expect to pay more for accommodation, make sure to book well in advance and be prepared for large crowds throughout the city all week long.

- Throughout the Plaza Machado are English-speaking volunteers offering tourist information for those who have questions. They wear marked blue collared shirts and are very helpful.

SIGHTS

Angela Peralta Theater
Located in Plaza Machado, this famous theater opened its doors in 1874. It has since been used for historical operas and cultural festivals. After a five-year renovation in the '90s, it is open to the public to view. Cost is 15 pesos.

Aquarium
Stroll through Mazatlan's large aquarium to see turtles, rare fish, seahorses, peacocks, coral and plant life - a nice way to spend an afternoon. Cost of admission is 90 pesos.

El Faro Lighthouse
Hike up to the second highest lighthouse in the world for a beautiful view of the city and sea – just don't forget your bug spray.

Cathedral Basilica de la Inmaculada Concepcion
Yes, you read that right: the cathedral of immaculate conception. This grand Roman Catholic Church can be spotted from most places in the city and is famous for its architectural design. A beautiful place to sit and reflect if you feel so inclined.

Olas Altas
Stroll through this area of town, west of Plaza Machado, to view colorful art galleries and quaint shops along cobblestone streets.

Malecón
Walk along the boardwalk to view the many landmarks along the way. Fisherman's Monument and The Sinaloan Family are great photo ops.

Sunsets

Sit on the beach to watch the sky turn orange and pink while the sun sets over the Pacific. Mazatlan's sunsets are famous and should not be missed!

ACCOMMODATION

Suitel 522 Eco Hostel

What used to be housing for local university students is now an ecologically conscious, clean hostel located three blocks from the beach. Rooms feel like mini apartments, and each comes with a fully equipped kitchen and free Wi-Fi. Continental breakfast included, laundry facilities available. Lovely courtyard and garden.

Cost: 250–500 pesos

Rio Presidio 522
Cross Street: Rafael Dominguez
Palos Prietos CP 82010
669-985-4140
info@suitel522.com
www.suitel522.com

Hotel Posada Los Tabachines

Basic, clean rooms are available here with Wi-Fi and private bath. This quaint hotel is situated one block from the beach and is staffed with friendly faces. All rooms come with a television and air conditioning. Suites with full kitchens available. 24-hour reception and security on premises.

Cost: 300–450 pesos

Rio Fuerte and Fracc. Telleria
CP 82017
669-982-6609
www.hoteltabachines.com

Hotel Posada La Mision

Clean, large hotel a few blocks from the beach in the Zona Dorada. Swimming pool, Wi-Fi, 24-hour reception. Rooms are basic but clean, with no TV or phone; friendly staff encourages guests to get out and enjoy the city, or simply relax.

Cost: 350 pesos

Ave. Camaron Sabalo #2100
CP 82100
669-913-2444
www.posadalamision.hostel.com

SHOPPING

Central Market

This giant open-air market is a great place to people watch, eat a meal and do some shopping. You can find everything from fresh baked goods, meat, seafood, produce, leather goods, handmade crafts and clothes.

Gran Plaza

Located in the Zona Dorada is a large mall with more expensive clothing and shoe stores. Those looking for a bargain can venture into the Wal-Mart. Gran in Spanish, grand in English.

Zona Dorada

Stores line the streets of this area of Mazatlan. Wander along to find handmade gold and silver jewelry, leather goods, Mexican blankets, pottery and more.

SAYULITA

"I came, I saw, I stayed." Backpackers and tourists have been heading to Sayulita for years. Local expats call it the vortex, because once you get here, you won't want to leave. This small town has a big personality – friendly locals, beautiful beaches, a tight-knit expat community, excellent shopping and cheap eats are only some of the things that keep people coming back.

Once upon a time it was a sleepy fishing village, but the famous surf break on the bay attracted surfers, tourists and expats looking to create a life in a foreign country. These days you can see kids running around freely through the plaza while live music plays and locals play volleyball as the sun goes down over the Pacific.

Delicious, cheap street food can be found all over town. You can find fish and meat tacos, tamales, fresh fruit, pastries, cake, empanadas, chips, *elote* (corn on the cob or in a cup with salt, lime and chile), crepes, churros, deep fried plantains, and the list goes on.

Spend your days eating, lounging in the sun or getting active; there's lots to do, depending on what you're into. Some events around town are only spread by word of mouth, so make sure to introduce yourself to hostel staff and locals to get in the know.

HOW TO GET THERE

Located about 45 minutes north of Puerto Vallarta, Sayulita is an easy bus ride from the city.

From Puerto Vallarta, hop on a bus in front of Wal-Mart. The bus you'll take will say Sayulita on the windshield. Cost per person is 25 pesos. The bus will drop you off just outside of town.

To enter Sayulita, walk across the bridge. The beach will be on your right, and town straight ahead.

To get to Wal-Mart from any point in Puerto Vallarta, get on a bus that says Wal-Mart on the windshield. Depending on where you are in the city, the bus will cost between 10–20 pesos.

You can also take a taxi from Puerto Vallarta to Sayulita, but the bus is safe, convenient and much cheaper. Negotiate a price with your driver before accepting a ride. Average rate should be around 600 pesos.

THINGS TO KNOW

• Sayulita is a small beach community, and everyone knows each other.

• Be respectful of the locals. If you meet someone, say hello the next time you see them in the street. This will go a long way.

• Locals survive slow summer months off money they make during the high season. Please remember to tip. The standard rate is between 10-15 percent, but if you receive excellent service, feel free to leave more.

• Don't go on the beach at night.

• Make sure to clean up after yourself, especially on the beach.

• Sayulita is safe, but as a general rule of thumb, don't walk long distances by yourself at night.

• Even if dogs don't have a collar, most have homes.

For information about anything and everything Sayulita, including vacation rentals, visit www.sayulitalife.com.

SIGHTS

Cemetario de Los Muertos
A short walk along the beach heading south past Villa Amor, you'll come to the cemetery where flowers and decorative tombstones are great photo ops. Keep walking past the cemetery and turn right to Playa de Los Muertos for a quiet beach day.

Playa Carrisitos
Hike through the jungle further south of town to a secluded beach where waves outnumber people. From Playa de los Muertos, follow the dirt road from the cemetery into the jungle and take the second right turn. The walk should take about 20 minutes.

Iguana Tree
Directly behind restaurant Tierra Viva is a famous tree where iguanas can be spotted and photographed.

THINGS TO DO

Surf or Stand Up Paddle Board
Take a surf or paddle board lesson or rent a board with any of the local surf schools. Luna Azul is quite popular, but several surf schools line the beach. Waves are generally small and great for beginners.

Horseback Ride
Take a tour through the jungle, along a beach or through town. Horses vary in size but are all well trained and cared for. Ask for Manuel along the beach for a guided horseback tour. Prices vary depending on number of horses, length and destination of tour.

Whale Watch
Chica Locca offers daily trips to nearby islands and beaches. Day trips include transportation to and from the boat, breakfast and lunch, all you can drink, snorkeling, paddle boarding, and if you're lucky, lots and lots of whale watching.

Cost: $75 USD

Yoga
Multiple yoga studios are sprinkled throughout town. Walk in to get more information about style and price, as they vary. Yoga on the beach is also available.

Salsa Dance
Salsa classes at Don Pedro's restaurant are available every Monday night from 7 p.m. Professional instructors will teach you the basics. Live Cuban band provides the tunes.

Cost for Salsa Class: 100 pesos
Cost of Entrance after 8 p.m.: 50 pesos

Open Mic Night
Local bands and tourists are welcome to share their music at Don Pato's Bar every Tuesday night. Stop in for a good show.

Cumbia Night at El Camaron
Popular with locals and tourists, Friday's cumbia night at El Camaron campground is a great place to meet people and dance on the beach until late night, or early morning, depending on your mood.

Fishing
Stop by Tigre's surf tent and ask about fishing rates. Mahi mahi, red snapper and roosterfish can be caught daily.

ACCOMMODATION

The Amazing Race Hostel
Brand new, colorful, clean and modern, this hostel has everything you could want – shared kitchen, swimming pool, comfortable common area, huge lockers, an outlet, light and shelf above every bed, and friendly staff. There's also a climbing wall, laundry facilities, Wi-Fi, BBQ, and cable TV. English spoken.

Cost: 195–220 pesos for dorm; 500–600 pesos for private room

102 Pelicanos St
Sayulita, Nayarit
329-291-3688
amazinghostel@usa.net
www.theamazinghostelsayulita.com

Casa Amistad Hostel Sayulita
Located one and a half blocks from the beach, this hostel has a great vibe – the shared, open-air dorm is on the second level. Book and music library, surf and boogy boards and snorkel equipment are all free to use during your stay. There's also a great terrace with hammocks, shared outdoor kitchen, and lovely owner, Coni, has many return customers. She'll even teach you Spanish if you feel so inclined.

Cost: 200 pesos; 10 percent discount when you stay for a week or more.

6 and 7 Manuel Rodriguez Sanchez
Sayulita, Nayarit
329-291-3804
lacroixsayulita@hotmail.com
www.hostelsayulita.com

Farmer's Market
Every Friday from 9 a.m. to 2 p.m., vendors set up along the river with organic produce, ready-made food, fresh salsas, coffee, flowers and snacks. Some favorites are tamales, Yerba Buena juice, Spanish tortilla, gluten-free quiche and turmeric iced tea.

Tiangis Sunday Market
This Mexican flea market begins across the street from the OXXO and continues down to the beach. If you spend a little time digging, you may be able to find some hidden treasures. Inexpensive underwear, clothes, shoes and kitchenware are available for purchase.

Street Artisans
All through town and along the beach artisans set up stands with their one-of-a-kind, handmade jewelry. Silver, gold, copper and feathers are popular. Take a walk around before you commit to a purchase – there is a lot to choose from!

Boutiques
Some are pricey, and some are quite reasonable, depending on what you're looking for, but all of the boutiques in Sayulita sell unique clothes, home décor, jewelry, leather goods, bikinis, shoes and jewelry. Take a day to window shop and we bet you'll fall in love with one thing or another, whether that be a freshwater black pearl necklace, hand made leather purse with fringe, authentic Mexican tiles, or a beach bag made out of recycled material with an image of the Virgen de Guadalupe.

PUERTO VALLARTA

Vallarta is a small town within big city limits. It's a beach-goers destination, but the city prides itself on having something for everyone – families, spring breakers, young, old, the gay and lesbian crowd, and yes, even you, solo female backpacker. People travel to PV from all over to go diving, deep sea fishing and sailing, but if none of that appeals to you, you can always get to know the ocean the old fashioned way and swim.

Hungry? There are tons and tons of restaurants. In fact, you may be busting at the seams by the time you leave. There is a wide variety of street tacos, 5-star fancy food and everything in between. You can't walk one block without running into at least five places to sit and have a snack, or a full on meal.

Nightlife here offers a wide variety of party options. There are clubs, sports bars, lounges, live music venues, a theater with live performances and pubs throughout the city. Interested in seeing an authentic mariachi band? Cuban salsa? Jazz? The most popular bars and clubs are located on the *malecón*, or boardwalk, and stay open until the wee hours of the morning. And with lots of budget accommodation options, it's no wonder millions flock here every year.

HOW TO GET THERE

If you're looking to explore the Pacific side of Mexico, Puerto Vallarta's international airport is a good place to land. They have daily flights from most international airports in the U.S. and Canada, and also to cities throughout Mexico. We've also found some great deals on flights from the west coast of the U.S.:

Gustavo Diaz Ordaz Airport (PVR)

If you're traveling light, you can take a public bus from the airport into town. Walk to the exit of the airport onto the main highway. You'll want to head to your right. Get on a bus that says 'Centro' to go downtown.

The main bus station, or the *Central Camionera*, is located north of the airport, at Calle Bahia de Sin Nombre 363, just off the MX-200 Highway. Inside, you can buy tickets to go north, south, or east, on first or second-class buses.

THINGS TO KNOW

- Local buses around the city are easy to use – they have posted on the front window where they're headed, and cost 6.5 pesos. Keep small change for the bus – they likely won't be able to break big bills. Once on the bus, hold on tight! Drivers will often start driving before they've given out change.

- There is a big gay and lesbian scene in Puerto Vallarta – clubs, resorts and even a gay beach. The community is very accepting of same-sex couples.

- Take a walk down the malecón (boardwalk) to see some street art – there are permanent statues along the beach, and some street artists making some quite impressive sculptures out of sand. Nightclubs along the malecón get busy late – usually around midnight.

- If you're into nightlife, do yourself a favor and go out one night in the city center. There are more locals here and you'll have just as much fun as you would in the hotel zone.

- Not everyone who does not look like a local is on vacation – there is an active expat community in Puerto Vallarta.

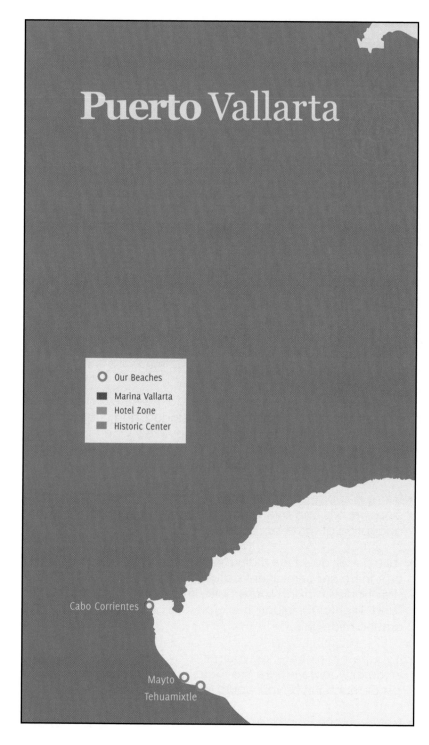

Puerto Vallarta

○ Our Beaches
■ Marina Vallarta
■ Hotel Zone
■ Historic Center

Cabo Corrientes ○

Mayto ○
Tehuamixtle ○

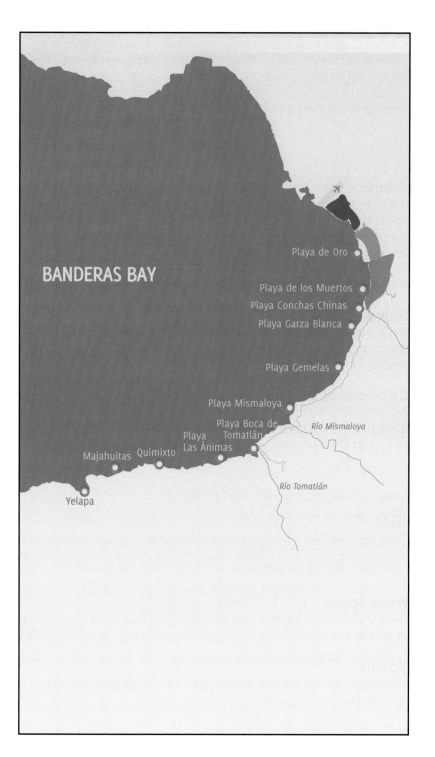

BANDERAS BAY

Playa de Oro

Playa de los Muertos

Playa Conchas Chinas

Playa Garza Blanca

Playa Gemelas

Playa Mismaloya

Playa Boca de
Tomatlán   *Río Mismaloya*

Playa
Las Ánimas

Majahuitas Quimixto

Río Tomatlán

Yelapa

- What used to be Old Town is now called the *Zona Romantica*, or the Romantic Zone. There are plenty of places to shop here, including a Sam's club, Wal-Mart, open-air markets, a shopping mall and boutiques, but you're not likely to get harassed by vendors on the beach.

SIGHTS

Yelapa
This sleepy beach town is nestled on the southern most tip of the Bahía de Banderas. It's mostly accessible by water. You can take a water taxi from Vallarta in the morning and be back by nightfall. It's a beautiful place to swim, lounge in a hammock, snorkel and parasail. It's also a nice change from the bustling city – there are almost no cars. For more information, visit www.yelapa.info

Teatro Vallarta
This theater offers a mix of live music concerts, operas and dance performances. It has the capacity to seat 960 people and is located in the center of the city.

Cathedral of Our Lady of Guadalupe
A beautiful church located one block from the malecón and beach. The bells chime all day on the hour, and it's a nice place to sit and take photos.

THINGS TO DO

Party
Your trip to Puerto Vallarta isn't complete without at least one night out on the town. Wear your dancing shoes! Clubs, discos and bars stay open late.

Water Sports
Dive, sail, deep sea fish, parasail and paddle boarding are all popular here.

Zip Line
Vallarta's background is lush jungle. Take a zip line tour to see a different side of the city.

ACCOMMODATION

Oasis Downtown Vallarta Hostel:

This quaint hostel is located in the center of downtown Vallarta, right next to the cathedral. It has a beautiful rooftop view, friendly staff, funky décor and is one block from the beach. Thursday is ladies night, where 30 pesos covers all you can drink with your fellow barhopping hostel goers. Shared kitchen and bathrooms, Wi-Fi and breakfast included.

Cost: 180 pesos for a bed in a shared dorm

Juarez 386
Puerto Vallarta, Jalisco
322-222-2636
info@oasishotel.com
www.oasishostel.com

Vallarta Sun Hostel

This popular hostel is located in the Zona Romantica, also known as old town, and is one block from the beach. Hand painted walls and pillowed seating fill funky common areas. Friendly English speaking staff is in-the-know about what to do around town. Some room have twin beds and double beds.

Book ahead for the female only dorm, as it fills up. Shared kitchen, Wi-Fi and discounted tours available.

Cost: 220 pesos for a bed in a shared dorm

Francisca Rodriguez 169
Puerto Vallarta, Jalisco
322-223-1529
www.vallartasunhostel.com

Oasis Hostel

This is the original location for the Oasis chain, and offers the same amenities as the downtown hostel, but it's a bit further away from the beach (15 mins.) and main attractions of the city. The hostel is comfortable, spacious and fun with a rooftop terrace, friendly staff, handpainted bathrooms and a free drink at check-in.

Cost: 180 pesos for a bed in a shared dorm

Libramiento 222
Puerto Vallarta, Jalisco
322-222-2636
info@oasishostel.com
www.oasishostel.com

SHOPPING

Paradise Plaza

There is a plethora of places to shop in Vallarta. Head to Paradise Plaza, the large mall in Nuevo Vallarta, for a mix of high-end stores, boutiques and handcrafts.

Mercado Municipal Flea Market
A good place to buy souvenirs. Beware that a lot of the vendors sell the same items. You'll see lots of ceramics, clothing, jewelry, handcrafts, leather goods and hand-woven stuff. Check out their backpack selection.

Rio Quale
Along the River Quale is a long stretch of vendors who are eager to make a sale. They have normal market stuff – jewelry, art, clothes, leather goods. It's a nice walk even if you chose not to buy anything.

Along the malecón are surf shops, boutiques and a mix of hand-crafts and trinkets.

There are several other stores throughout the city. Take a walk through downtown and the Zona Romantica to find shoe stores, clothing outlets, fabric stores and everything in between.

Sand castle artist on the beach in Puerto Vallarta

ACAPULCO

Acapulco was once one of the most visited resort towns in all of Mexico, but drug-related violence has increased in recent years, which has affected the tourism and stability of the area. Many cruise ships have stopped visiting Acapulco, and it's really not a place we can recommend you travel to alone right now, or with a group of girlfriends, for that matter. There are so many other more beautiful parts of Mexico, and several other towns with beautiful beaches. The water in Acapulco can be dirty, and the constant harassment from locals trying to get you to buy something becomes really exhausting.

Set on Acapulco?
If none of this matters to you and you're gung-ho on Acapulco, consider splashing out a bit to stay in a nice hotel like Fiesta Americana, listed below.

Kingdom Youth Hostel
The only budget hostel in town is not actually in Acapulco at all. It's nearby in Puerto Marques', but it only costs about 10 pesos to get into town. Kingdom Youth Hostel is arguably the best place to stay while in Acapulco, with friendly locals, picturesque scenery and a chill vibe. Hostel shuttles can take you to the airport.

Cost: Varies. Roughly 100–150 pesos.

Carre Tara 4
Puerto Marques #104
Acapulco

Fiesta Americana Villas
These beachfront Villas are among the most recommended to us. Choose from either rooms or private villas. Rooms are nice and clean, staff is friendly and the location is great, but it comes at a price! This is not a budget backpacker's joint.

Cost: 1,200+ pesos

Av. Costera Miguel Alemán No.97
Fracc. Club Deportivo
744-435-16 00
www.fiestaamericana.com

CENTRAL

CENTRO

Small towns in the central region of Mexico are quaint and stunning, with grand cathedrals, mountain views, botanical gardens, natural hot springs, universities that look like palaces and streets so small and windy you'll get lost in a sea of colorful houses. Streets are full of music, cafes and art galleries line sidewalks, and it's possible to see each town almost entirely on foot.

TOP ⭐ PICKS

Best Way to Spend an Afternoon:
Hot Springs in San Miguel de Allende

Best Place to Take Spanish Classes:
San Miguel de Allende

Best Bar Hopping: Guanajuato. Start at Los Lobos or Bar Fly and work your way around downtown.

GUANAJUATO

Guanajuato is a place of music. Young people from all over the country, plus some international students, come here to study theater, the arts and other subjects at one of the country's most famous public universities.

For this reason, the narrow streets are filled with 20-somethings at almost any hour of the day. To pass the time, locals perch on steps in front of the Juarez Theater, sit on benches that line the various plazas, talk, people watch and wander around.

This colonial town has a rich history. The Spanish discovered silver and gold here in the 18th century, and at one time, Guanajuato was home to the richest silver mines in the world. The mines are still in operation today, and you can visit them, along with a slew of other interesting historical buildings, museums and cathedrals, including the house where Diego Rivera was born.

The city was built in a deep valley; the historical center is located at the base, with multicolored houses scaling the surrounding mountains. Because of its unique geography, some of Guanajuato's streets can be more like alleys, the most of famous being *El Callejon del Beso*.

The easiest way to navigate Guanajuato's narrow cobblestone streets is by foot. Sidewalks here are made for one person, and some aren't even wide enough for cars, let alone buses. You'll spend a lot of time weaving through foot traffic and stepping off curbs to make way for others, but that's part of its charm. If you feel claustrophobic reading that, don't; there are plenty of places to stretch your legs – almost every hostel has a rooftop terrace, and multiple plazas in the city offer wrought iron benches under shady trees, perfectly designed for taking a break.

HOW TO GET THERE

Guanajuato city is located in the state of Guanajuato, which is between three and four hours by bus from Guadalajara. It borders the states of Jalisco, Michoacan, San Luis Potosi and Queretaro.

There is one main bus station, or *centro de camiones*, in town. We recommend taking a taxi to your accommodation – it should cost between 40–50 pesos.

THINGS TO KNOW

- Since Guanajuato is a town of music and young people, it is also a town of noise. Be aware that if you chose to stay in the

MAP OF GUANAJUATO

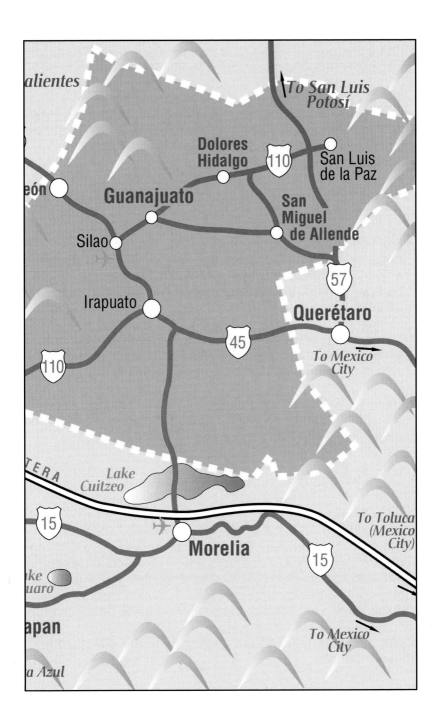

Centro Historico, it will be loud at night. Keep in mind that if you head downhill, almost all streets lead to the Centro Historico.

- There is a big nightlife scene in town, and most bars don't get crowded until 12 p.m. or later. Bars will usually stay open as long as there are people inside. Two favorite local spots are Bar Fly, which plays reggae music, and Los Lobos, the rock bar.

- Spanish classes are offered at multiple private schools throughout town, but it is much cheaper to take classes at the University of Guanajuato, with just as good, if not better, instructors.

- Most of the main sites can be visited within a few days, but don't be surprised if you want to stay for a while. Guanajuato is quite charming, and the people are very friendly. It won't be hard to make friends, especially if you go out to a bar and strike up a conversation.

- Cobblestones streets can be uneven. Wear comfortable walking shoes, and watch your step. Also, the altitude here is high. Make sure to drink lots of water to avoid altitude sickness.

- Tourist kiosks are located at various plazas and main intersections throughout town. Staff are very helpful but don't always speak English. Be patient.

SIGHTS

Teatro Juarez

Inaugurated in 1903, this theater is quite famous, and for good reason – both the exterior architecture and interior detail are exquisite. Inside is all red and gold, lined with wood. Walk upstairs to view the old smoking salon, where men and women would gather during intermission to talk and have a cigarette. After the tour, take a seat outside on the front steps to people-watch.

Open: Tuesday-Sunday: 9 a.m.–1:45 p.m.; 5 p.m.–7:45 p.m.
Closed: Monday

Cost: 35 pesos regular admission; 15 pesos students
Additional 30 pesos if you would like to take photos

Museo y Casa de Diego Rivera
Diego Rivera, one of the greatest Mexican painters and muralists, spent his first six years of life in this house, which was converted into a museum in 1975. View his home and several works of art, including oil on canvas, sketches, cubism and nude portraits and beginnings of some of his murals.

Cost: 20 pesos general admission; 5 pesos for students

Basilica de Nuestra Senora de Guanajuato
Visit this beautiful cathedral to see the Virgen de Guadalupe, which was a gift from Spain after silver and gold were discovered in the mines. You are welcome to photograph the crystal chandeliers that line the ceilings, pillars, statues and shrines, but please be respectful of those who came to pray; keep your voice low and your flash off, if possible.

Jardin de la Union
This central plaza is located right across from the Teatro Juarez, and is a great place to hear music during the evenings. Wrought iron benches line the garden; large trees provide shade from the hot sun. Restaurants and cafes line the outer portion of the plaza. Sit and have a meal and listen to the mariachis and other local musicians, who play for everyone.

Museo Iconografico del Quixote

This large museum dedicated to the infamous character created by Miguel de Cervantes is free on Tuesdays and is also quite impressive. There are drawings, bronze statues, ceramic figurines, sculptures and paintings in 16 rooms split between two floors. All of the work is by Mexican artists, and some pieces are upwards of 40 years old.

Open: Tuesday-Saturday, 9:30 a.m.–6:45 p.m.; Sunday, 12 p.m.–8:45 p.m. Closed: Monday

Cost: 30 pesos regular admission; 10 pesos students; free on Tuesdays

Callejon del Beso

The tiniest of the tiny alleyways in Guanajuato is the *Callejon del Beso*, where balconies from across the street almost touch one another. The story goes that back in the day, when two lovers lived across from each other, they would kiss each other from across the alley – hence the name.

Museo de las Momias

See some real life mummies at this creepy museum at the edge of town. Because of the high mineral content in the soil and the extremely dry weather, some bodies in the local cemetery were naturally mummified in the 19th century. They were discovered when bodies needed to be dug up so more could be buried. You can now visit over 100 of them in the museum. Weird, right?

Open: Daily, 9 a.m.–6 p.m.

Mino y Templo la Valenciana

You can visit this mine that is still in operation today to see miners working to extract silver, gold and other minerals. You can also visit the nearby temple, La Valenciana, which was constructed in the late 18th century.

Open: Daily, 8 a.m.–6 p.m.

ACCOMMODATION

Al Son De Los Santos

Our favorite hostel in Guanajuato is an easy 10-minute walk to the center, which means it's quiet at night when you want to go to sleep! The large, female-only dorm is clean, comfortable and has a spacious bathroom inside the room with a great shower. Rooftop terrace, 24-hour reception, shared kitchen, Wi-Fi and quaint common spaces included.

Cost: 180 pesos for a bed in a shared room

San Sebastian 94
Zona Centro, Guanajuato
473-731-3368
alsondelossantos@hotmail.com
www.alsondelossantos.com

Hostel Guanajuato

This basic, clean hostel is also located in the Centro Historico, next to Santo Café (a great spot for tasty, cheap eats). The large, shared dorm has a separate bathroom that is located outside the room. The hostel offers a nice common space inside with a TV, and there is a shared kitchen and Wi-Fi.

Cost: 100 pesos for a bed in a shared room

Calle Campanero 14
Centro Historico, Guanajuato
473-732-9567
www.hostelguanajuato.mex.tl

SHOPPING

Mercado Hidalgo

At the local open-air market, you can find sweets, clothes, textiles, ready-made food, produce and hand-made crafts, split between two stories. Be aware that it can get quite busy during the afternoons.

SAN MIGUEL DE ALLENDE

San Miguel de Allende is the Mexican motherland for artists and expats, and it's not hard to figure out why. The appeal of this little mountain town is simple: there are multiple outdoor activities available to pass the time, a mild climate year-round with a heavy dose of sunshine, and an active expat community. Thousands of tourists come per year, many of whom decide to stay and tap into their creative side.

This is not a place to be in a hurry. The serene, laid-back attitude of San Miguel is part of its appeal, and what's helped make it famous, along with the fact that it's a UNESCO World Heritage Site. Spend the late afternoon in the botanical gardens, watching the sun go down over hundreds of species of Mexican plants and cactus, or head to the hot springs for a swim. Or you could always walk around town, photograph unique doors and buildings, peruse art galleries and then sit in a café along the main plaza for a coffee and a snack. You get the idea.

Don't speak Spanish? Not a problem. Since so many foreigners call San Miguel home, it's one of the few places that is easily navigated with English alone. If you'd like to learn to speak

Spanish, however, there's a class for that. In fact, there's a class for just about anything you'd like to learn. Mexican cooking? Yoga? History? Art? You name it, it's available - for a price.

In fact, pricey is a good word for San Miguel where food is concerned. You can find street tacos of course, but restaurants are usually upscale, and often somewhat expensive by Mexican standards. Dinner in a sit-down setting will cost you anywhere from 80-300 pesos, respectively. But there are exceptions to every rule, and shared kitchens in all the hostels we recommend. Happy cooking!

HOW TO GET THERE

San Miguel is a big tourist destination, and buses arrive hourly from several different areas of the country. Generally speaking, it's nestled in the mountains between Guadalajara and Mexico City in the state of Guanajuato.

There is one main bus station in San Miguel, called the *centro de autobuses*. It should cost between 30–40 pesos to take a taxi into the center of town, depending on your final destination and bargaining skills. It may be possible to walk to your hostel from the bus station – ask hostel staff specifics before you arrive. They are happy to help!

THINGS TO KNOW

• There is a great English newspaper that includes information about the city, upcoming events and classes, called *Atención*. It costs 10 pesos and can be purchased at the public library, which also has books in English that can be checked out.

• A full-moon ceremony takes place once a month at the botanical gardens around 6 p.m. It's a unique experience, with chanting, cleansing of the spirit and offerings to the universe. The ceremony is held in English and Spanish.

• San Miguel is a small, walking town. Cobblestone streets can be uneven. Watch your step, and wear comfortable shoes. Altitude is high. Make sure to drink lots of water to avoid altitude sickness, and limit the amount of sun you get. Always wear sunscreen and if you have one, wear a hat.

- Temperatures drop at night. Don't get caught in the cold! Bring layers to keep warm.

- Visitors are welcome to visit and photograph the local churches, but not during mass and other services. Remember that you are visiting a religious place of worship. Respect those who are there to pray by keeping your voice low.

- Getting the "gringo rate," or higher rate in cabs, is not common, but happens. Make sure to negotiate a price of a taxi before entering the car. You are always free to say no thank you and walk away if the price is too high.

- Locals in San Miguel love an excuse for a festival. Don't be surprised if you stumble upon one during your stay.

SIGHTS

Parroquia
This beautiful pink, seemingly gothic cathedral is located in the Plaza Principal, also known as the Jardín, and is the central focal point of the city. The inside of the cathedral is just as beautiful as the outside, with wood carvings, vaulted ceilings, fresh flowers and gold pillars. Lights illuminate the exterior at night.

Plaza Principal
Also known as the Jardín, or garden, this plaza is considered the center of the city. Wrought iron benches line the exterior and it's a great place to sit and people watch.

Botanical Gardens
You'll want to bring your camera for this excursion. Wetlands, various kinds of rare Mexican plants and cactus and art line the many walking paths. Go with a few hours to spare as it takes some time to see everything. Guides are available, but it's easy enough to grab a map at the entrance and walk the paths yourself. It's best to go in the early morning or late afternoon – don't forget sunscreen and water! Cost is 40 pesos.

La Gruta Hot Springs
These hot springs are located on the outskirts of the city and should not be missed! There is a cave you can swim in, indoor and outdoor pools, plus a bar with food service. Bring a towel,

bathing suit, and snacks if you're looking to save money.

Parque Juarez
This pleasant park is a short walk from the Plaza Principal, and is a great place to go for a walk or run with the rest of the locals. It's shaded by trees, and local artists set up here selling their work.

Historic Museum of San Miguel
If you're interested in learning about the history of San Miguel, that is, when and how it was settled, and how the town has come to be what it is today, you should stop into this museum. A collection of art, armor, foundation documents and information can be found on the first floor. The second floor is a recreation of the Allende family home, and what it would have looked like in the 18th century.

Bellas Artes
The main art school in town is always free to visit. Murals, changing exhibits and a lovely garden can be found inside. Ask about art classes if you feel so inclined.

El Mirador
This spectacular lookout point gives you a panoramic view of the city. It's within walking distance of the center, but it's quite a hike. We recommend taking the bus, which can be taken from a few points in the city, depending on where you're coming from. Ask hostel staff where the nearest location is, and make sure to tell the bus driver that you're going to the Mirador.

Mercado de Artesanias
This market sells a large collection of handmade crafts, art, silver and leather goods. If you're looking to buy gifts, this is a good place to do it, but if you're heading to Mexico City or Guadalajara from here, we recommend doing your shopping there. Goods are less expensive in bigger cities.

Art Galleries
It seems that every street in San Miguel is lined with art galleries and cafes. If you're looking to take some great photos, wander the streets that surround the Jardín and snap away!

Hostal Punto 79

This hostel is brand new and offers one of the best locations in the city, a block from the central garden. The space itself is a remodeled early 20th century home. Beds are comfortable and the rooms are clean. Ask about promotions and you may receive a discount. Wi-Fi, shared kitchen, 24-hour security and funky décor included.

Cost: 175 pesos for a bed in a mixed dorm

Mesones 79
Centro Historico, San Miguel De Allende
415-121-1034
reservaciones@punto79.com
www.punto79.com

Hostal Alcatraz

This hostel offers lots of information on what to see and do throughout your stay, along with tours of the city and surrounding areas for an additional fee. There is a nice central common area, and they also offer Spanish classes with professional instructors if you feel like brushing up on your Español. Shared kitchen, clean bathroom outside the shared female dorm, BBQ, Wi-Fi, and lockers. Reception is open from 9 a.m.-9 p.m., but guests have access to enter and exit 24 hours a day.

Cost: 130 pesos for a bed in a shared dorm

Relox 54
Centro, San Miguel de Allende
415-152-8543
alcatrazhostel@yahoo.com

Hostel Inn

This hostel looks more like a hotel once inside, and has room for upwards of 40 people. There are four shared dorms, a large, outdoor area and garden, shared kitchen, Wi-Fi, BBQ, and 24-hour reception. Laundry facilities also available. Friendly staff are willing to answer any questions you may have.

Cost: 130–150 pesos for a bed in a shared dorm, depending on day of the week. (Weekends are more expensive)

Calzada de La Luz 31-A
Centro, San Miguel de Allende
415-154-6727
www.hostelinnmx.com

SHOPPING

There are tons of goods and art available for purchase in San Miguel, but if you're on a budget, we recommend you save your money for one of the bigger cities. Since there are so many tourists here, things are likely to be more expensive than they would be in, say, Mexico City.

Mercado Ignacio Ramirez

A good place to stock up on produce and other foods. We recommend you sit in the food court section for a *licuado*, or smoothie, blended with the fruit of your choice for around 20 pesos. Delicious.

GUADALAJARA

The second largest city in Mexico has some of the most exquisite architecture in the country, and is the self-proclaimed fashion capital. With no metro system, buses can be somewhat difficult to navigate, but people are friendly and more often than not offer advice to a solo girl on the road. The Zocalo is full of people, street performers and photo ops, but be careful in the market – it's dense and very crowded.

TOP  PICKS

Best Place to Spend an Afternoon:
Hospicio Cabanas

Best Art Galleries: Tlaquepaque

Best Neighborhood for Nightlife:
Chapultepec

GUADALAJARA

The second largest city in Mexico is full of musicians, artists, writers, students, artisans, intellectuals, and, in general, creators. It is a blend of old and new ways of being – a Spanish style colonial house recreated into an art gallery or boutique, or a tattooed

GUADALAJARA

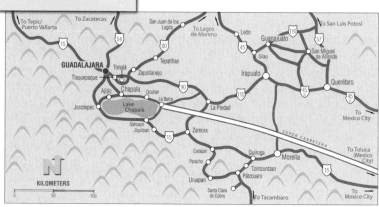

GUADALAJARA MAIN STREETS, HOTELS

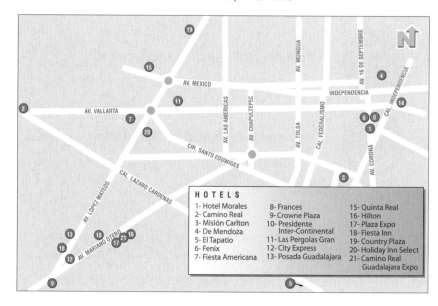

HOTELS

1- Hotel Morales	8- Frances	15- Quinta Real
2- Camino Real	9- Crowne Plaza	16- Hilton
3- Misión Carlton	10- Presidente	17- Plaza Expo
4- De Mendoza	Inter-Continental	18- Fiesta Inn
5- El Tapatio	11- Las Pergolas Gran	19- Country Plaza
6- Fenix	12- City Express	20- Holiday Inn Select
7- Fiesta Americana	13- Posada Guadalajara	21- Camino Real
		Guadalajara Expo

GUADALAJARA ATTRACTIONS

1 Cathedral	7 San Juan de Dios Church	13 Templo Expiatorio
2 Degollado Theater	8 Templo de San Francisco	14 Plaza de la Liberación
3 Palacio de Gobiernno	9 Templo de Aranzazú	15 Plaza Guadalajara
4 Museo Regional	10 Templo de Santa Monica	16 Plaza de Armas
5 Instituto Cultural Cabañas	11 Templo de San Felipe Neri	17 Parque Morelos
6 Mercado Libertad	12 University of Guadalajara	18 Parque Revolución

GUADALAJARA WALKING TOURS

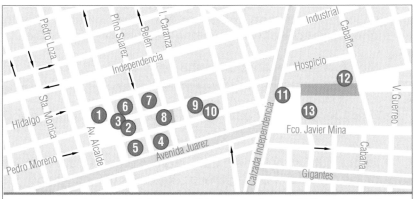

1 Palacio Municipal	4 Palacio de Gobierno	7 Museo Regional	10 Plaza de los Fundadores
2 Cathedral	5 Plaza de Armas	8 Plaza de la Liberación	11 Plaza Tapatia
3 Plaza Guadalajara	6 Rotunda de Los Hombres Ilustres	9 Teatro Degollado	12 Instituto Cultural Cabañas
			13 Mercado Libertad

musician sitting next to a traditional mariachi on the bus, for example. It is an array of diverse faces and places, and if you're up for a little adventure, you'll never get bored here.

The energy of the city is somewhat intense – buses, cars and taxis create a sea of traffic, especially in the Centro Historico, where most of the main sites and markets are located. Foot traffic is also dense, though there is usually a bench or step to sit on if you need a break. These come in handy more often than you might think.

Some of the most famous and important architectural buildings in the country are located in Guadalajara. A vast mix of styles and fusions make up the city's architectural DNA, and there are many variations on each style, depending on the building. Think texture, pillars, high ceilings, detail, arches, symmetry and bold lines. It's easy to spend an afternoon (or two) taking photographs admiring the incredible magnitude and vibe of each one.

And oh, the food. Anything your stomach desires is at your fingertips, from traditional Mexican fine dining to street vendors. If you're sick of tacos at this point, don't worry—one of the perks of being in a big city is the diversity of cuisine.

THINGS TO KNOW

- Guadalajara is the second largest city in Mexico and there are a ton of things to do. If you have time, spend at least five days here to get to know it well. Centro Historico can easily be explored on foot – monuments, plazas, museums, the cathedral, theater and market are all within walking distance of one another.

- Most tourist attractions are in the city's historic district – you will save time and money on transportation if you stay in this area.

- Buses generally cost between 6–10 pesos, depending on your destination.

- Check out Chapultepec: This is a great area to stay in – much of the nightlife and art galleries are in this neighborhood; the vibe is young and the streets are safe.

- Make sure you have room on your camera's memory card and space in your suitcase for a few souvenirs.

- Always keep a close eye on your belongings, no matter where you are. If you choose to carry a purse, make sure it has a zipper. Hold your purse close to your body in crowded, tight spaces – especially the market - and keep money in separate places. You can never be too careful!

- Fashion is a big industry, and most people dress on the nicer side of casual, no matter what they have planned for the day. For that reason, this is a great place to photograph street style. Closed toed, sturdy shoes are preferable for daytime excursions. You will do a lot of walking.

Other Tips

- If you plan to go out at night, take some toilet paper with you. A lot of bars and clubs will run out.

- Many taxis use meters, but only if you ask. Metered rides are generally less expensive than flat rates.

- Many citizens of Guadalajara are of Spanish and European decent – don't be surprised if you see a blonde haired, fair-skinned woman speaking rapid Spanish.

- Guadalajara is one of the more difficult cities to navigate if you don't speak Spanish. Brush up on your vocabulary before arriving if possible.

HOW TO GET THERE

There are two main bus stations in Guadalajara:

Old
This bus station makes trips to nearby towns and suburbs that are more or less within 60 miles of the city, like Tequila and Chapala, and is considerably smaller than the new bus station. Ask your hostel staff for directions by local bus, otherwise hop in a taxi and ask to use the meter.

New
This is the long distance bus station has seven terminals and will take you just about anywhere you want to go. It takes about 40 minutes to arrive via taxi from the city center, depending on

traffic. Make sure to get there an hour before your departure time to buy tickets and choose your seat.

Libertador Manuel Hidalgo International Airport
Has domestic and international flights arriving daily. Check with your hostel about pick-up rates, as their prices will most likely be cheaper than a taxi.

SIGHTS

Centro Historico

Catedral Metropolitana
Construction of this much-visited Catholic cathedral began in the 16th century. Admire its stunning architecture from a seat in Plaza de Armas before going inside to see giant pillars, stained glass windows, depictions of saints and La Virgen de Guadalupe, and locals speaking in hushed voices to priests. A beautiful place to sit and reflect. Feel free to take photos.

Teatro Degollado
The first opera was held here in 1866, and the building is a great example of neoclassical architecture. The theater holds 1,025 spectators and opera, classical dance, contemporary and folklore shows, plus cultural events and performances by the Philharmonic Orchestra of Jalisco, are held regularly. Inside is a depiction of Dante's Divine Comedy painted on the ceiling painted by Jacobo Galvez and Gerardo Suarez. Visiting hours of the theater sometimes change, but are usually between 12-2 p.m., Mon-Sat.

Guadalajara Palacio de Gobierno
The government building is another colonial, architectural gem, and is historically important – slavery was abolished here in 1810. Go inside to see murals by Jose Clemente Orozco that depict the abolishment of slavery by Manuel Hidalgo. Free to enter.

Hospicio Cabanas
This grand building on the far end of Plaza Tapatia used to be a shelter for homeless children run by the church, but is now a museum protected UNESCO World Heritage Site. Jose Clemente Orozco, a famous muralist, painted the entire interior, ceilings and all, supposedly with one hand. Paintings are inspiring and you can lay on benches inside for hours, each moment noticing something

different. It's pretty trippy and was our favorite afternoon activity. Cost is 70 pesos for non-nationals.

Mercado Libertad
This is one of the largest markets in Mexico, and it spans three floors. Inside you can eat lunch, purchase handmade crafts, movies (pirated), clothes, shoes, any kind of leather good you can imagine, jewelry, weapons, watches, sunglasses, and the list goes on and on. Hallways can get quite narrow and crowded, so make sure to hold on to your purse. It is open from 6 a.m.–8 p.m. daily.

Plaza de los Mariachis
Mariachi music was born in Guadalajara, and these days, you can sit in this famous plaza and hear bands play throughout the afternoon and early evening. Restaurants line the streets; sit and have a meal if you feel so inclined.

Other Areas

Tlaquepaque
This is a small town at the southeast tip of Guadalajara, and it's worth the trip! Art galleries line walking streets, artisans and sculptures are everywhere, and it's a nice break from the hustle and bustle from the city. A taxi should cost between 150–200 pesos, or ask your hostel staff for directions to take the bus, as you will need to transfer.

Chapultepec
This area of the city is somewhat small, and is packed with art galleries, fashion boutiques, restaurants, cafes, bars and nightlife. Live music can be heard almost anywhere, and the vibe in this area of the city is young and trendy. On Saturdays, there is a small, charming street market. Rent a bike to discover all the neighborhood has to offer.

TAKE A DAY TRIP TO TEQUILA

If you're interested in finding out more about the agave plant and how tequila is manufactured, take a day trip to—you guessed it—Tequila! Sample the original Mexican Margarita in a town full of local distilleries that produce the only liquor that can truly be called tequila. Be sure to do a bit of research beforehand. Most distilleries are open to the public but some require advance booking. You can also choose to do an organized tour from Guadalajara, or, you could just take the bus out there (6–10 pesos) and see what you find.

ACCOMMODATION

Hospedarte Hostel Guadalajara Centro

This hostel has everything you could want: organized activities for getting to know the city, a large common area, shared kitchen, continental breakfast, Wi-Fi, free bicycle rentals, big lockers and maps of the city. A great place to stay if you're looking to mingle. Discounts available for students and Hostel International members. Each room has a balcony and the female-only dorm has a huge full-length mirror.

Cost: 170 pesos for a bed in a shared dorm

Calle Maestranza 147
(at the corner of Lopez Cotilla)
Centro Historico, Guadalajara
333-562-7520
info.chapu@hospedartehostels.com
www.hospedartehostel.com

Hostel Tequila Backpackers

This clean hostel located about 15 minutes from the heart of the city's Centro Historico has a pool (which will come in handy after walking the city all day), Wi-Fi, free bike rentals, large patio and common areas. Tours in and around Guadalajara also available, and there's also a restaurant and bar on the first floor with a daily happy hour. This is a great hostel if you're looking to meet people and exchange some stories. Credit cards accepted.

Cost: 180 pesos for a bed in a shared dorm

Avenida Hidalgo 1160
Zona Centro, Guadalajara
333-825-1326
hostel@tequilahostel.com
www.tequilahostel.com

Degollado Hostel

This basic and spacious hostel is in the heart of the city's historical center. You are literally steps from the Degollado Theater, and each room has a terrace – some with a view. Continental breakfast, shared kitchen, Wi-Fi and friendly staff included.

Cost: 180 pesos for a bed in a shared dorm (female only available); 400 pesos for private room.

Calle Degollado 20 (between Calle Morelos and Calle Pedro Moreno) Centro Historico, Guadalajara
333-613-6331
www.degolladohostel.com
info@degolladohostel.com

Hospedarte Hostel Chapultepec

The second hospedarte location offers the same amenities in a different area of the city. Very helpful staff will be happy to offer advice on things to see and do, and the spacious patio out front is a great place to sit and have a drink. There's also a garden with hammocks for lounging.

Cost: 170 pesos for a bed in a shared dorm

Calle Efrain Gonzalez Luna 2075 (half a block from Chapultepec Ave.)
Colonia Americana, Guadalajara
333-615-4957
www.hospedartehostel.com

SHOPPING

Mercado Libertad
You can find just about anything you could ever need or want here. Located in the Centro Historico.

The Streets of Centro
For artisan goods, walk the streets of centro – it will be most packed on weekends. Jewelry, ceramics, and interior décor can be purchased. Feel free to barter.

Plaza del Sol
A large outdoor mall that holds boutiques, department stores, restaurants and cafes. To get there, take any bus with 'Plaza del Sol' written on the windshield. Confirm with the bus driver of your destination before hopping on.

OAXACA

Food, beach, mountains, cities – in that order. Oaxacan cuisine is as diverse as the state itself. Start in Oaxaca City to see one of the most intricate and ornate churches in all the country, popular plazas and go shopping in one of the many open-air markets, continue on to San Jose del Pacifico to get a glimpse of the cloud forest and surrounding mountains, then stay in Puerto Escondido and Mazunte to see some serious surf.

TOP ⭐ PICKS

Best Hostel:
Buena Onda in Puerto Escondido

Best Alternative Lodging:
Posada del Arquitecto in Mazunte

Best Street Food:
Tlayudas inside the 20 de Noviembre market in Oaxaca City

OAXACA CITY

The city of Oaxaca is diverse– walking along narrow streets and through dense open-air markets, you'll hear indigenous dialects mixed with Spanish as you browse vendor stands full of intricate woven, beaded and hand-made textiles. There are seemingly endless food stands and restaurants offering traditional Oaxacan

OAXACA STATE

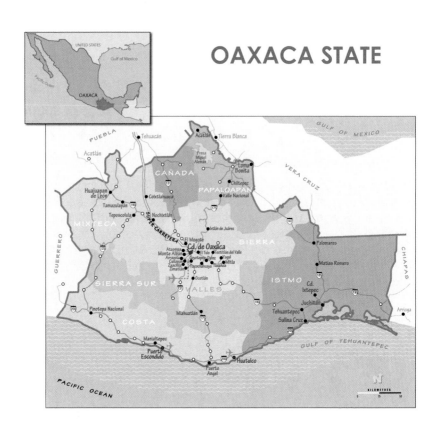

OAXACA COAST

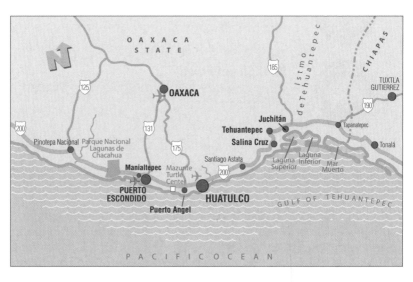

OAXACA CITY

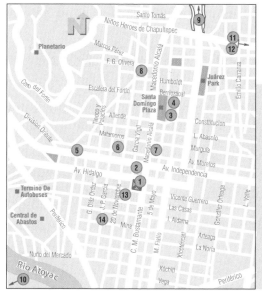

1 Plaza de la Constitucion
2 Catedral
3 Iglesia y ex-Convento de Santo Domingo
4 Centro Cultural St. Domingo
5 Basílica de la Soledad
6 Museo de Arte Prehispánico "Rufino Tamayo"
7 Museo de Arte contemporáneo de Oaxaca (MACO)
8 Museo Casa de Benito Juárez
9 Fuente de las Siete Regiones
10 Monte Albán Archaeological Site
11 Mitla Archaeological Site
12 Yagul Archaeological Site
13 Mercado Benito Juárez Maza
14 Mercado de Artesanías

OAXACA CITY SURROUNDING AREA

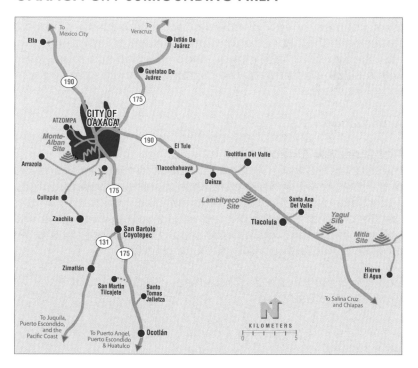

food and drinks – *mole*, cheese, chocolate and coffee, just to name a few. One thing is for sure – you'll never go hungry here. In fact, you'll probably finish each day so full that you'll be content to stay in and relax rather than go out and party.

The city center is alive and full of people who are selling their wares, shopping and taking some time out in the Zocalo to do nothing at all but enjoy the sunshine. Nearly 300,000 people of indigenous and mestizo descent call the city of Oaxaca home. The Spanish arrived here in the 16th century, and there are numerous museums, cathedrals, churches, temples and a few archaeological sites where you can admire art and architecture from both pre-Hispanic, Spanish-influenced and modern culture. Wander, eat, shop, and eat some more. The food is delicious, the people are warm, and the climate is mild, making for a very pleasant experience in the capital city.

HOW TO GET THERE

Airport
Oaxaca's airport is international, though it will most likely be cheaper to fly to Mexico City. To get from the airport to the city, take a combi van to your hostel or accommodation. Kiosks are stationed in the airport, and it's much more affordable than a taxi, though it will take longer, since you'll be in a shared ride with multiple passengers. The combi van should cost no more than 100 pesos.

Airport Code: OAX

First Class Bus Station
The first class bus station in Oaxaca is about a mile from the Zocalo and, in theory, within walking distance to some accommodations. If you have a lot of luggage or the distance sounds too far, taxis are stationed outside the bus terminal for your convenience. The ride should cost no more than 50 pesos. First class bus companies that travel to Oaxaca: ADO, OCC and UNO.

Calzada Niños Heroes de Chapultepec 1036.
Cross Street: 5 de Mayo

THINGS TO KNOW

There are tourist kiosks set up throughout the center of the city, and more often than not, employees and volunteers speak English. Ask their advice on where to go, how to get there, and any other questions you may have. They have an answer for everything, and usually a map and directions to go along with it.

• The city is dense and sidewalks are narrow, especially around the Zocalo, where food and vendor stands are set up daily. You'll probably get stuck behind some slow walkers. Accept that things take a little bit longer here than they do in other places, and plan accordingly.

• Dress conservatively in the city. No matter how hot it gets, locals keep it quite covered up, usually wearing long pants or skirts, and long sleeves. If you wear a short skirt, shorts, or show cleavage, you will get a lot of looks and unwanted attention from men.

• The food in Oaxaca is very distinct from the rest of the country. You must try mole, Oaxacan cheese, tlayudas, chocolate, coffee and mezcal at least once during your stay.

• Combi vans are the most affordable way to travel from Oaxaca City to the coast. There are multiple companies throughout the city that can take you where you need to go, usually for 200 pesos or less.

• Unless you plan to see the ruins of Monte Albain or another point of interest outside the city, it's unlikely you'll need to leave the center. You can take buses around the center, but we found that is was easier to walk, plus walking ensures you'll see it all at your own pace. Wear comfortable shoes.

There are tons of museums, churches, temples and points of interest in Oaxaca. We have listed our favorites below, but you'll probably stumble upon many more on your walks throughout the city.

Monte Albain

This Zapotec archaeological site located outside of Oaxaca is a UNESCO World Heritage Site. A local bus can take you round trip for 40 pesos, and the ride takes about 20 minutes one-way. Entrance fee is 57 pesos. Be advised that the last bus back to the city leaves at 3:30 p.m., even though the ruins stay open until 5 p.m.

Open-Air Markets

There are multiple open-air markets where you can easily spend an entire afternoon wandering, eating and shopping. Descriptions of a few of the best markets are below in the shopping section. If you plan to shop, try to take small bills with you; vendors usually don't have change for 500 peso bills.

Zocalo and Cathedral

In the Zocalo, or the main square in the center of the city, you can see live music most Monday, Tuesday, and Sunday evenings. Restaurants and cafes line the exterior. Stop for a snack, meal, or drink. The cathedral is located on the northern end of the Zocalo. Paintings inside date back to the 16th century, and there are more than 10 chapels inside dedicated to different saints.

Santo Domingo de Guzman Church

This is the most magnificent church we saw during our entire trip through Mexico. The interior walls, alters and ceiling are all gold and wood, with intricate designs and decoration carved in practically every inch of space. The chapel inside is also completely comprised of gold. The church itself dates back to the 16th century.

Centro Cultural Santo Domingo

Directly next door to the church is a restored former convent that has been turned into a museum, and guides visitors through an elaborate, multi-floor recreation of Oaxaca's history. Inside are artifacts from pre-Hispanic times, information on surrounding plants and animals, the arrival of the Spanish and the progression into modern day Oaxaca. 57 pesos to enter.

Rufino Tamayo Museum of Prehispanic Art
This museum features pre-Hispanic art collected by Rufino Tamayo, one of Mexico's most famous artists. The museum is closed on Tuesdays, and open from 10 a.m. – 3 p.m.

Arte Contemporaneo, MACO
This museum holds temporary modern art exhibits from Mexico and around the world. When we visited, they were hosting an exhibit with work from contemporary Spanish artists. Entrance is 20 pesos.

Botanical Gardens
Unfortunately, no visitors are allowed to enter the botanical gardens without a guide, and guided tours in English are only available once a day and are more expensive than the tour in Spanish. Check at the entrance for times and rates, as they vary.

ACCOMMODATION

There are hundreds of accommodation options in the city – hotels, hostels, bed and breakfasts, vacation rentals and motels, and new places pop up all the time. If you pass by one that looks inviting, stop in and ask for rates and a tour.

Casa del Sol Hostel

The spacious dorm room offers really comfortable beds and drapes to close your space off from the rest of the room, and tiled, pretty bathrooms. The garden and common areas are lush with bouganvillia - you'll feel like you're staying at a boutique hotel rather than a hostel. The shared kitchen closes in the early evening, so if you plan to cook, do so in the afternoon. Tours can be arranged at the hostel, and it's located on a quiet street within walking distance to the Zocalo and other main points of interest in the center of the city. Although this is the prettiest place to stay, it's small and very quiet, which can make it harder to meet people.

Cost: 160 pesos for a bed in a shared dorm.

Constitucion 301
Centro, Oaxaca
951-514-4110
reservas@casadelsol.com.mx
www.hostalcasadelsol.com.mx

Casa Angel Youth Hostel

This new, large hostel is very clean and social, with a rooftop deck with a view of the city. Staff hosts BBQs on the roof over the weekends so guests can mingle and eat together. Staff is bilingual and very helpful. Wi-Fi, 24-hour security, information on tours and classes offered in Oaxaca (language and cooking, among others), and the place is usually full of backpackers. The hostel is located on a hill on the outskirts of the center of the city, which provides a great view, but a longer walk to the Zocalo and other points of interest.

Cost: 140–170 pesos for a bed in a shared dorm.

Tinoco y Palacios 610
Centro, Oaxaca
951-514-2224
info@casaangelhostel.com
www.casaangelhostel.com

Casa de Don Pablo Hostel

This hostel is quiet, and within walking distance to the Zocalo, main markets, and other points of interest in the center of the city. The 10-bed dorm is the cheapest option, and while beds aren't the most comfortable we've ever slept on, the rooms and shared bathrooms are clean. 24-hour reception, hearty breakfast included, Wi-Fi, shared kitchen, friendly staff (though not all are bilingual), and open common areas include a rooftop view of the city. Beer and snacks available for purchase at the front desk.

Cost: 145 pesos for a bed in a shared dorm.

Melchor Ocampo 412
Centro, Oaxaca
951-516-8384
lacasadedonpablo@yahoo.com.mx
www.casadedonpablo.com.mx

SHOPPING

There are several open-air markets in Oaxaca:

Benito Juarez
This place a little bit of everything – ready-made food and produce, clothes, shoes, leather, flowers, handcrafts, jewelry, textiles and more. It can get very crowded very quickly, and aisles are narrow. Bring some patience and a calm demeanor, as you'll need to say 'excuse me' and 'no, thank you' several times as you wander through this dense market.

20 de Noviembre
This is the best place to come for a cheap, authentic Oaxacan meal - the entire market is dedicated solely to food. There are sections for meat, sweets, chiles, chocolate, cheese and bread, among other things, and about half of the market is made-up of ready-made food stands and restaurants. Be advised that patrons can be somewhat aggressive in their quest to get you to sit down and eat with them, as opposed to their neighbor. Ask to see the menu before you commit. It's also a good idea to check out which are the most popular with the locals – they know best.

Mercado de Artensania
The artisan market is full of color – woven rugs, pillow cases, purses, tapestries, blankets and pouches, along with leather goods, hand-made jewelry, pottery and other beaded textiles. This is a great place to take photos and buy a few gifts if you're in the mood to shop, but take a full lap around the market before you commit to a purchase – there are multiple aisles full of handmade goods, and once you see it all, you can make an informed decision on what you want to buy.

Mercado de Abastos

This market is where large shipments of produce come in. Chefs and restaurant owners get here early to stock up. It's unlikely you'll need anything from this market that you can't find at the others that are located in the center.

There are also popular weekly markets in pueblos around the city. Ask your hostel staff or an employee at a tourist kiosk for information and directions on when to go and how to get there. We heard great things about the Sunday Tlacolula Market.

Take a walk around the center and you're sure to stumble upon pop-up markets and vendors on the street, especially towards the botanical gardens along Macedonio Alcala and 5 de Mayo. There is an endless amount of things to see and buy in Oaxaca, just don't exceed your budget before you get to Chiapas, if you plan to go!

Shopping in Oaxaca is great and affordable, but we found that markets in Chiapas are less expensive than those found here. Unless you're looking to buy something specific from Oaxaca, save your money for San Cristobal de Las Casas.

PUERTO ESCONDIDO

Puerto Escondido is completely obsessed, infatuated and saturated with surf. Home to the Mexican pipeline and some of the biggest waves in the world, people from all over come here to compete and test their skill. For this reason, swimming in a few of the beaches in this hidden port is seriously discouraged, so much so that if you try to swim at Zicatela beach, you'll be stopped by lifeguards.

Puerto Escondido, once a small fishing village and port, is now home to nearly 50,000 people. This big city on the Pacific has dramatically different beaches and neighborhoods. A few miles east or west will lead you to a quiet bay where you can swim and float without worry, while monstrous waves crash and command respect at the next. Walk uphill into the center of town to find it bustling with locals, working and shopping, or walk down to the beach along a windy staircase to find it empty except for a few visitors working on their tans.

The appeal of this place, other than the surf, of course, is that it is a big city with all the amenities you could ever want or need – large supermarkets, easy public transportation, an airport and first class bus stations for easy access, great restaurants and nightlife, but the beach community maintains a small town vibe. Meet your bliss and a bunch of serious surfers in Puerto Escondido, just don't forget your sunscreen!

Photo courtesy of Hot Toddies Unlimited

PUERTO ESCONDIDO

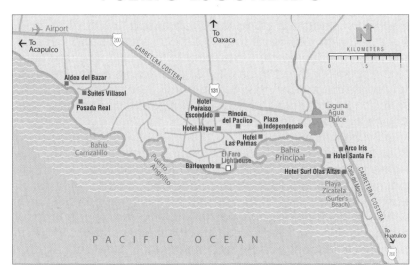

PUERTO ESCONDIDO AREA

From San Jose del Pacifico
Take the combi van to Pochutla. From Pochutla, you will need to ask for the local bus that goes to Puerto Escondido. Your driver will be able to direct you to the station. It's about 5 blocks from the drop off point, and buses leave about once an hour.

From Oaxaca by First Class Bus
The ADO first class bus leaves daily. It's about 10 hours to the coast from the city by first-class bus, and more expensive than taking a combi van, but it's also much more comfortable. If you don't want to waste a whole day on the bus, buy a ticket for an overnight trip.

From Oaxaca by Combi Van
Combi vans are much less expensive than the bus, but they're also less comfortable. The road is windy and narrow through a mountain range, and the ride takes about 6 hours. If you tend to get motion sickness, be sure to buy some anti-nausea pills at the pharmacy before you leave.

The cheapest way to get around Puerto Escondido is by colectivo. Shared red and beige cabs and covered trucks charge 5 pesos for a ride. Each car has their destinations written on the front windshield.

If you're heading to La Punta from the ADO bus station, cross the main road and wait for a colectivo that says 'La Punta' on the front.

A regular, private taxi from La Punta to the center or vise versa should cost no more than 30 pesos.

Airport
Puerto Escondido's airport is about 3 miles from the center of town, but since it's a smaller airport, flights can be somewhat expensive.

Airport code: PXM

THINGS TO KNOW

• The biggest waves and surf contests are during the summer.

Photo courtesy of Hot Toddies Unlimited

- Swim with caution! Zicatela beach is home to the Mexican pipeline and some of the biggest waves in the world. This beach is for pro surfers only, and no one swims here. If you try to swim the lifeguard on duty will stop you. That doesn't mean you can go take a walk down it and admire the swells that challenge even the most skilled surfers though. Beachfront bars and restaurants offer great views.

- Unless you want to surf, you'll want to stay on or near a beach where you can swim. We chose La Punta because it's quiet, beautiful and has some delicious, cheap restaurants. It's also a popular hangout for local surfers, and easily accessible by public transportation. Be advised that there are no ATMs along La Punta. If you plan to stay in this area of the city, stop at an ATM beforehand.

- Shop in the center of town for the best deals. Stores along the beach can be more expensive, since they cater mostly to tourists.

- Street signs are uncommon in Puerto Escondido, so you'll need to rely on directions from locals to get around. Ask a few people before heading too far to ensure you're going the right way. Taxi drivers usually know how to get to hostels and hotels, but look up directions online beforehand just in case.

- Most of the partying goes on over the weekends, but there are some local bars along Zicatela beach that are open during the week. Ask about ladies night and cash in on some free cocktails.

- La Punta is a great place to surf, but can get crowded.

- Carizalillo is a great beach to learn to surf and is the best for swimming. It's a little out of the way, but there are restaurants and surf instructors that will keep you full and occupied.

- The hottest month of the year on the coast of Oaxaca is May. Avoid going to Puerto Escondido during this time if possible. Temperatures can get up to 130 degrees Fahrenheit.

- Wear lots of bug spray and sunscreen.

- Never leave home without your flip-flops. The sand here gets so hot that your feet will burn and then blister if you're left in the heat with nothing to stand on.

- The main grocery store in the city is called Super Che, and is similar to Costco. You can buy everything you need here. This is a good place to shop for items you need, but might have forgotten – sunscreen, bug spray, a towel, hat, beach blanket, etc.

- Colectivos fit up to six people, with two passengers sharing the front seat. It can be cramped, but it's the most economical way to get around.

- Men outnumber women. Don't be surprised if some local boys hit you on more than once.

For more information, check out *www.puertoescondidoinfo.com*

············· THINGS TO DO ·············

Beach
There are several beaches in Puerto Escondido, but not all are good for swimming. Playa Carizalillo was our favorite to swim in, as it's really calm and inviting. It's accessible only by a walking trail that leads down a long winding staircase. You can also swim at La Punta, Puerto Angelito, and Manzanillo. Zicatela is beautiful for a sunset walk, but not for swimming.

Surf

Surfers could be at any beach, depending on the waves that day. Popular surf spots are La Punta, Zicatela and Carizalillo.

Laguna de Manialtepec

This lagoon is about half an hour from Puerto Escondido, and if you're there during the right season, you can go for a night swim with phosphorescent algae. The sparkly plankton lights up when disturbed by movement, so your whole body will be lit up in bright blue and green colors when you jump in and swim. And the best part – the water is warm. It's remarkable, to say the least! We went on a trip with Lalo Ecotours. *www.lalo-ecotours.com*

The phosphorescent plankton phenomenon is unpredictable, so ask about it before you book. Other things to see at the lagoon are huge mangrove forests, fish and several species of birds. Day trips include trips to essentially private beaches, stand-up paddle boarding and expert tour guides who can point out rare species of animals. Puerto Escondido Eco Adventure Tours also comes recommended. *www.ecoadventurespuertoescondido.com*

Day Trips

See sea turtles, dolphins, birds, other marine life and otherwise inaccessible beaches on a boat trip during the day. Walk to Playa Principal where boats are stationed. You'll get offers for day trips from captains. Negotiate a price before getting onboard.

Deep Sea Fish

Puerto Escondido is a fishing community. Experts dive, deep-sea fish, and take their boats out daily. Walk along Playa Principal and talk with local fisherman about taking a trip, or to buy the fresh catch of the day.

Day Trip to Chacahua

Chacahua is a unique community of lagoons and beaches, with focus on conservation of sea turtles and crocodiles, and surfing of course. The people are of African descent, so they are darker than the average Mexican. Chacahua can be difficult to get to on your own, as you'll need to take a bus, then a boat, and then another bus to get there from Puerto Escondido. Talk to your hostel staff about day trips and tour operators. Visit *www.lagunasdechacahua.com* for more information.

Nightlife

There are several bars along Zicatela beach. Most are packed on the weekends, though there are some places to go during the week if you're itching to get out and about. Head here for dinner and you're sure to get stopped by promoters who pass out fliers for whichever bar happens to host ladies night that evening.

ACCOMMODATION

Cabanas Buena Onda

This is one of those places you never want to leave. Located right on the sand at La Punta, the staff is multi-lingual and extremely helpful, providing information on tours and how to get around town. Start your day at the beach, then head in for a nap in one of the 10 hammocks in the common area, then across the street for lunch, and then back to the beach for sunset. Wi-Fi, open-air kitchen, clean rooms, friendly faces and good vibes. There are private cabanas, dorm rooms, and areas to pitch a tent if you have one. This hostel is very popular, mostly due to word of mouth – there is no website or online presence. Call in advance to book.

Cost: 100 pesos for a bed in a shared dorm

La Punta Zicatela
Puerto Escondido, Oaxaca
954-582-1663
buenaondazicatela@live.com
www.buenaonda.hostel.com

Tower Bridge Backpackers

This place has a reputation for being a very social hostel, and is quite popular with backpackers, which makes it easy to mingle and make friends. They have a bar, spacious swimming pool, BBQ, a travel desk, Wi-Fi, 24-hour reception, shared kitchen and are within walking distance to Carizalillo and Bacocho beaches. The owner is very friendly and likes to mingle with guests. Great common area with a pool table and games to keep you occupied, and surfboards and boogie boards for rent.

Cost: 80 pesos for a bed in a shared dorm

Oceano Antartico #1
Puerto Escondido
954-582-0823

Osa Mariposa

This small, new hostel is also located at La Punta. It's made up of bungalows, and situated in a quiet residential neighborhood two blocks from the beach. A tropical fruit garden is a beautiful place to lounge, and the place is quiet and clean. They also offer tours around the city, a free book exchange, kitchen, common areas, locally grown, vegetarian meals for purchase and a mezcal bar. Since this place is new, make sure to have some directions on hand for your taxi driver, in case they don't know where it is. Signs are posted once you turn off the main highway.

Cost: 100 pesos for a bed in a shared dorm

Privada De Cancun
Colonia Brisas De Zicatela
954-110-8354
info@osamariposa.com
www.osamariposa.com

SHOPPING

Benito Juarez Market
In the center of Puerto Escondido, there is a large, open-air market with tons of small food stands, artisans and vendors selling everything from fresh fruit to handmade leather goods and woven rugs. Take a trip to the market for a delicious lunch or dinner and some shopping.

Shopping Along Zicatela Beach
There are several boutiques, surf shops and other stores along Playa Zicatela. Some are pricey, but you can definitely find a bikini or pretty beach gear to take home. Spend an afternoon window shopping and wandering in and out of stores before the sunset, but just to be safe, leave your credit cards at home.

Super Che is the best place to go grocery shopping, and to buy other practical necessities – sunscreen, beach gear, etc. There's also an ATM inside. It's located in the center of town, just off the main highway.

Photo courtesy of Hot Toddies Unlimited

MAZUNTE

This is Mazunte – a small beach community in Oaxaca, home to endangered sea turtles, heavy waves and quiet nights. The bohemian community here is much less surf-obsessed than that of neighboring Puerto Escondido, and more focused on nature and conservation. Many artisans flock to the small beach town, weaving and creating handmade jewelry and goods to sell along beaches throughout the day.

The town itself is very small, with two main roads to the beach. There are restaurants, posadas, cabanas and shops along both. There is a produce store along the main road, next door to the pharmacy, where you can buy all of your fresh fruits and veggies. Restaurants can be found along the beach and throughout town, offering typical Mexican dishes and some international food. Wander around, lounge in hammocks, sunbathe, hike and make some new friends as you get accustomed to the slow pace.

Really... what's the rush?

HOW TO GET THERE

Public Transport
The road to Mazunte is off the main highway in between Pochutla and Puerto Escondido. Coming from either city, tell the bus driver you're going to Mazunte and need to get off at "las cruces de San Antonio," or "*el crucero*." Ask the driver to let you know when to get off. You'll know you're there when you see an OXXO and a Pemex gas station on the highway. Wait in front of the OXXO for a truck, van or taxi that turns off the main road on the way to Mazunte. The ride should be about 15 minutes to town from the OXXO and should cost between 5 and 10 pesos.

If this sounds quite loose and informal, that's because it is. Sometimes, travel in Mexico involves a little patience and good faith. There are no big bus companies that go straight to Mazunte, so to get there, you'll need a little of both.

Taxi
You can also take a taxi straight to Mazunte from Pochutla or Puerto Escondido. Pochutla is about 30 minutes from Mazunte.

Puerto Escondido is about an hour.

From Pochutla, a private ride in a taxi should cost around 100 pesos.

From Puerto Escondido, a private ride in a taxi should cost no more than 300 pesos.

THINGS TO KNOW

- There are no ATMs in Mazunte. Bring enough cash for the length of your stay, otherwise you'll have to take a trip to Pochulta to pull out more pesos.

- Currents can be strong here, and big waves are common. Make sure to use caution when swimming. Look for flags before you dive in – red means currents are particularly strong in that area.

- Wear lots of bug spray. There are a lot of mosquitos, and they like new skin.

- Temperatures are hottest in the month of May. Avoid the coast of Oaxaca during this time if you can. When we were there, it was 125 degrees. Wear lots of sunscreen and drink lots of water!

There are many places to stay in Mazunte, and on your walk to the beach you'll pass countless posadas, cabanas for rent and vacation rentals. Stop in if neither of the below accommodation options sound like a place you'd like to stay, or if one catches your eye. Mazunte sustains itself on fishing, tourism and your generosity. It's not a bad idea spread it out a little bit.

SIGHTS

Centro Mexicano de Tortuga – Turtle Reserve and Gardens
Sea turtles are endangered in this area, and this turtle sanctuary houses several species of turtles that are in danger of extinction. Here you can visit the animals and view the work the people

of Mazunte, Oaxaca and Mexico are doing to ensure their preservation.

Hours: Hours vary depending on season. Check their website for more info.

Cost: 27 pesos

01-958-584-3376
www.centromexicanodelatortuga.org

Boat Trips
Tour leaders walk around town selling boat tours that include a visit to watch as sea turtles hatch on the sand and make their way to the ocean, if it's the season. On your excursion, guides will also point out dolphins, birds, whales and other sea life, and take you to a few nearby beaches. Expect to pay around 300 pesos for the day.

Punta Cometa Hike
There is an easy hiking trail above Playa el Rinconcito beach to Punta Cometa where you can watch the sun set. It's a beautiful walk, and once you're on top, you can capture views of Mazunte's beaches, see the currents and waves form, and watch some master fisherman work on the rocks below. Bring your camera, water and a sarong to sit on.

Beach
There are two main beaches in Mazunte. Playa El Rinconcito, next to the point, is the most popular for swimming.

Yoga
Yoga studios are located throughout Mazunte, and some people come here solely to participate in retreats that last between a few weeks to a month—sometimes longer. Hridaya Yoga comes recommended. The studio in Mazunte is called El Corazon, and if you chose to participate in a retreat, they have lodging on the grounds for students. *www.hridaya-yoga.com*

Posada del Arquitecto

This place is our No.1 recommendation for Mazunte. There are a few options for where to stay in the posada – there's a shared dorm, private rooms and 'estrella' beds, which are hanging double beds with mosquito nets on top of the property, attached to a open palapa under the stars with a view of the sea. The restaurant and café downstairs is a popular beachfront hangout. Check out the board in front of reception for information on nightlife and things going on around town. Free Wi-fi and large lockers.

Cost: 60–100 pesos a night, depending on the season, for a bed in a shared dorm or a hanging bed under the stars.

To get to the posada, turn right off of any of the main roads and head towards the beach. Ask for Playa El Rinconcito, and you'll run right into the posada.

info@posadadelarquitecto.com
www.posadadelarquitecto.com

Palapa El Mazunte

Just east of the Posada del Arquitecto on the west end of Playa Mazunte is Palapa el Mazunte. There is a restaurant on the beach in front of the palapa, which offers a variety of seafood and typical Mexican fare. You can rent a basic cabana, pitch a tent or rent a hammock to sleep in. Very laid back vibe right on the water. If you chose to camp or rent a hammock, there is a separate room where you can lock up your valuables.

Cost: Cabanas start at 150 pesos; 30 pesos for camping; 50 pesos to rent a hammock.

Palapa El Mazunte is located on Playa Mazunte. Take a walk down the beach and you'll see it on the east end of the beach, towards the point.

SHOPPING

Mazunte's artisans congregate around La Posada del Arquitecto and set up stands in front of the posada's restaurant. Here you'll find handmade jewelry, leather goods, feather earrings, rings, necklaces, clothing and more. Walk around before you commit to a purchase, and if you're not sure, take a day to think about it. They will most likely be in the same spot tomorrow.

SAN JOSE DEL PACIFICO

Nestled in the mountains about halfway between Oaxaca City and the coast lies the quiet town of San Jose del Pacifico. Many backpackers stop here on the way between the beach and the city, and for good reason – the trip is a long six hours along a windy mountain road that can cause all sorts of nausea. If you're not prone to motion sickness, the ride won't be an issue, but if you skip San Jose, you'll miss out on alluring hiking trails, peaceful sunrises and sunsets and the famous wild mushrooms that grow along hillsides throughout the rainy season.

The appeal of this little mountain town is of course, nature. Hiking trails run through thick patches of trees, huge maguey plants, out-of-the-way casitas and mountains that stretch out for miles on their way to the ocean. Many *temazcales,* or ancient sweat lodges, in the area offer a chance to experience the pre-Hispanic sweat lodges ancient Mesoamerican civilizations used to cleanse the body, spirit and mind, and accommodation is very reasonable. Stop for a day or two to get to know the alternative lifestyle of those living in (and visiting) the Oaxacan mountains.

HOW TO GET THERE

You can get to San Jose del Pacifico from Oaxaca City for less than 200 pesos. Once you arrive, it's much cheaper to take a *combi,* or a van, from the city to the coast, rather than a bus, and vise versa. Vans pass straight through San Jose del Pacifico to get to their final destination (usually Pochutla or Oaxaca City). You will get dropped off on the main highway near an internet café and coffee shop. The town is quite small, and locals are friendly. Ask for directions to your accommodation. None should be more than a 10-minute walk at most.

Ask your hostel staff where you can buy a ticket to get to San Jose del Pacifico from Oaxaca City or the coast. There are multiple companies. If you tend to get car sick, we recommend picking a window seat towards the front of the van.

THINGS TO KNOW

- It gets quite cold after the sun goes down. You'll need some warm clothes – layers are best – and you'll also want to shower during the day.

- Psychedelic mushrooms are common in the area. We do not ever recommend taking drugs in Mexico, but you may get offered some during your stay. If you do decide to take them, make sure you're with a group of people and use common sense. Don't go off on a trail alone, and stay hydrated.

- Small food markets are open during the day along the main road, but they tend to close early. Do your food shopping in the morning or afternoon.

- Temazcales are open daily. A temazcal is an adobe structure, similar to a sweat lodge. Make sure to drink a lot of water the night before your sweat, and to stay hydrated during and after the experience.

- Come prepared for some quiet time. You can buy beer at local stores, but there are seriously limited places to go out at night.

This is a great place to take a time-out and relax, but you won't need to stay in San Jose for more than a few days to see it all—unless you want to, of course. There are tons of cabanas all over San Jose. Some homes are even opened up with rooms for rent. If neither of the below two accommodation options sound right for you, when you get out of the van, just look around – signs for new posadas and cabanas pop up all the time.

THINGS TO DO

SWEAT IT OUT IN A TEMAZCAL

Temazcal
According to the temazcalero we spent some time with, a temazcal is similar to a pre-Hispanic church. This is where the indigenous would go to pray and participate in religious ceremonies with a shaman. Oral traditions were passed down from generation to generation, and while some of it was lost when the Spanish conquered Mexico, temazcales are still prevalent throughout Oaxaca and some parts of Chiapas.

Bring a bathing suit, towel and cloth or hand towel to wipe sweat from your face once inside the adobe structure. Hot rocks are used to create heat, and you'll sweat a lot. Be sure to stay very hydrated before, during and after. We recommend walking to town and asking around for a temazcal, rather than going with those who promote them at Catalina's posada. You'll have a more comfortable experience in the temazcales in town. We also recommend asking how many people will participate on the day you choose – the more people, the better. Do not go if it will just be you, or you and one other person; instead, wait for another day.

Hike
There are multiple hiking trails in and around San Jose. Make sure to bring water, sunscreen and your camera. You will likely spot some birds, plants, animals and views that you'll want to capture.

Practice The Art of Doing Nothing
San Jose is a great place to kick your feet up and reflect on your experiences thus far. Sleep in or get up early to watch the sun rise over the mountains. Have a coffee and write, read, take photos. Pick a trail and walk for a while, talk to some locals in town, buy a few things to make dinner. Take a nap. Watch the sun set. Check in with friends and family at home. Ease into the slow pace of things here – there is no need to be in a rush. When you feel rested and ready to move on, walk down to town and buy a ticket to get to the coast or Oaxaca City.

A Temazcal

Posada Dona Catalina

This house in the mountains into a popular backpacker hostel where everyone is welcome. Their clientele is quite diverse, and the décor is funky. Characters from all over the world (artisans, hippy-types, yogis, backpackers, locals) come here to relax on the terrace, which has an incredible view of the valley and mountains, share stories in the common room and take a break from city life. Be prepared that there is no hot water, but the place is clean, comfortable and social. If you have a choice, pick a twin bed in the common room, otherwise you may end up sharing a queen-size with someone. Simple breakfast included.

Cost: 50 pesos per night for a bed in a shared room.

There is no telephone or address here, so you'll need to ask for it. Walk up the paved hill across from the internet café and keep to your left. The posada is a green, two-story house on your left side.

La Puesta del Sol

Simple, private cabanas with hot water all day long, a queen size or double bed and beautiful views. There's also a restaurant on the property, internet and information on temazcales in the area and other local activities. La Puesta is located off the main road and is very quiet. There are TVs in some of the cabanas. If you're ready to take a break from hosteling, this is a good place to stay without breaking the bank.

Cost: 200 pesos for a basic private cabana. Prices go up depending on amenities.

You can call ahead here to the cell phone listed, or just walk up from the main road. Ask for directions at the internet café. It is about a 10-minute walk from where the van will drop you off.

951-596-7330
www.sanjosedelpacifico.com
sanjose@sanjosedelpacifico.com

SHOPPING

San Jose isn't really the kind of place you come to shop and there's nothing here to shop for. Enjoy the downtime and give your pocketbook a rest!

CHIAPAS

Known for its agricultural wealth and biodiversity, Chiapas is also famous for its indigenous cultures and handcraft markets. There are countless day trips you can take from San Cristobal de las Casas to see waterfalls, canyons, rivers, indigenous communities, coffee plantations, and some of the most stunning ruins in the country at Palenque. Give yourself at least a week in Chiapas; longer if you have the time. You'd be surprised how easily the days pass you by.

TOP ⭐ PICKS

Best Shopping:
Santo Domingo Crafts Market in
San Cristobal de las Casas

Best Place to Sit and People Watch:
Any of the restaurants along Real de
Guadalupe in San Cristobal de las Casas

Best Waterfalls: Agua Azul

SAN CRISTOBAL DE LAS CASAS

Walk up and down cobblestone streets passing colorful buildings, detailed wrought iron and wooden doors, graffiti, street art and small squares and plazas. You'll most likely find yourself gravitating to the international restaurants, boutiques, open-air markets and storefronts that line sidewalks in San Cristobal, and consequently heading to the ATM more times than you anticipated. This city is full of art, textiles, color, nature, and surrounding communities that still operate within traditions that were established thousands of years ago, before the threat of colonization.

Interested in learning about Mayan medicine practices? How amber is extracted from the earth and turned into jewelry? How cacao was harvested and turned into chocolate? Seeing a valley of flowers, or taking a boat ride through a canyon to view alligators, monkeys and birds where the indigenous offered themselves to the gods rather than be colonialized by the Spanish? What happened during the Zapatista movement, and how it's affected modern culture in Chiapas? This small town is full of culture and history, and is the perfect home base to explore Chiapas. Give yourself ample time to see everything you want, and a few days to explore the layers you weren't expecting to discover.

HOW TO GET THERE

The first class bus station, Terminal Cristobal Colon, is located at the south end of town, along Avenida Insurgentes. Major bus lines are ADO and OCC. To purchase bus tickets in San Cristobal, head to the ADO ticket office along Real de Guadalupe. If you're walking towards the Zocalo, it will be on your right hand side.

THINGS TO KNOW

Walking down the streets of San Cristobal, you're likely to hear multiple languages. Some you'll recognize – Spanish, English, French, Hebrew, Italian – others you won't, because they're indigenous languages, specific to the region of Chiapas.

According to the 2005 national census, the indigenous population of Chiapas makes up about 22 percent of the state's total population, and many come to San Cristobal to sell their handmade goods to tourists at the main artisan market. San Cristobal is, in our opinion, the best and most affordable place to shop.

• Real de Guadalupe is a pedestrian-only street, and runs right into the Zocalo, or main square.

- San Cristobal is small and completely walkable once you're situated in the center. Wear comfortable shoes.

- The Zapatista Revolution began in San Cristobal's Zocalo, and Zapatista communities are located throughout Chiapas. You'll see Zapatista slogans, images and paraphanalia on clothes, bags and street art throughout the state.

- All streets are one way, and most do not have traffic lights. Cars operate on a 1 to 1 system, much like an unofficial two-way stop sign – one car passes while another waits, and vise versa. Pedestrians do not have the right of way.

- Indigenous men and women still wear traditional clothing, which is elaborate and conservative. Keep yourself covered up, even if it's hot outside, to avoid stares and unwanted attention.

- It gets cold at night, since you're in the mountains at a high elevation. Bundle up with layers after the sun goes down.

- There are tons of international and vegetarian restaurants in San Cristobal – while we were there, we discovered a tea house that serves large, delicious salads, a falafel restaurant, Italian food, traditional Mexican fare of course, Argentine steaks, a vegan restaurant and tons of coffee shops with delicious deserts. Ask for recommendations or just wander into places on your own. Many of the restaurants we mentioned are on or around Real de Guadalupe.

- Sidewalks are narrow, and usually only allow space for one or two people.

- The further north you go in San Cristobal, the more crowded it is. On your way to the Mercado Municipal, you may get over-whelmed by the change in density. Only take what you need to this market. A big bag is a not recommended. The market is packed full of people, and getting your body through the crowd is challenging enough.

- Want to book a tour? Travel and tour agencies offer free information on day trips and things to do all in and around San Cristobal. They also offer transport across the border to Guatemala.

- There are lots of places to go out in San Cristobal, and there is a large number of young people who either live here or are passing through. Some popular nightlife spots are Revolucion Bar and mezcal bars around Real de Guadalupe. Many have live music at night – follow your ears.

- You'll get asked for money multiple times a day by the young, old, male and female. Give a few pesos every once in a while if you can, and remember that many of the people asking for money survive on tourism and your generosity.

- Stay in a hostel with hot water.

THINGS TO DO

Mundo Medicina Maya
This museum is very interesting and gives visitors an inside look into the traditions of Mayan medicine, including childbirth, the role of midwives, family, medicinal plants and temazcales. 20 pesos to enter.

Na' Bolom Museum and Gardens
This Museum and garden was founded in 1951 by the famous archaeologist Frans Blom, one of the first people to explore the jungle and Mayan communities in Chiapas, and his wife, Gertrude Blom. The institute is dedicated to Mayan traditions, and is a tribute to the couple who won the Nobel Peace Prize for their work with the indigenous population of the Lacadona Jungle. There is also a café inside the institute and a library. 40 pesos to enter.

Markets
Detailed descriptions of San Cristobal markets are in the shopping section below, but a trip to the city wouldn't be complete without a visit to a few of them. Bring small bills and your camera to capture the color and texture of artisan and food markets.

Jade and Amber Museums
If you're interested in learning how these precious minerals are mined and extracted from the earth and then sold, traded and turned into jewelry, visit the jade and amber museums.

Chocolate and Coffee Museums
Learn about how chocolate and coffee were first discovered, harvested and traded during pre-Hispanic times. You can also do a tasting of the chocolate and coffee made in the Chiapas region once you're done exploring each museum.

Zocalo and around
The Zocalo is a great place to sit and have a coffee, tea or snack and people watch. The main cathedral is located on the north side of the plaza, and live music can be heard on special occasions and weekend nights.

Day Trips:

San Juan Chamula and Zinacantan
San Juan Chamula and Zinacantan are two important Mayan communities in Chiapas and Mexico, and visitors come daily to see the blend of Mayan tradition inside San Juan Chamula's church. Inside the church, animal sacrifices and other pagan religious traditions are practiced, and it's a very interesting experience, to say the least. You can go on your own by hopping in a combi van at Avenida General Utrilla and Edgar Robledo, or go with a tour group.

Village of Zapatistas
Zapatista communities allow visitors, as long as you bring your passport and are not a doctor, lawyer or journalist. You'll need to ask around for a tour or how to get there, as buses do not run daily to these remote areas.

Lagos de Montebello

If you're looking to get off the beaten path, as they say, take a trip to the national park of the lakes of Montebello, where you can swim in crystal blue and green waters in any one of the 60 lakes. There is also a Mayan ruins site inside the park.

Canyon del Sumidero

Take a boat trip inside this magnificent canyon to see rare species of birds, crocodiles and monkeys. Once inside, your guide will show you a shrine to the Virgin of Guadalupe placed high in a cave, surrounded by flowers and candles.

Cascadas de Agua Azul and Misol-Ha

Day trips to Palenque first stop at the waterfalls of Agua Azul and Misol-Ha. You can swim in the crystal clear water at Agua Azul, and if you walk up far enough, you'll see indigenous women washing clothes in the traditional fashion.

ACCOMMODATION

Posada del Abuelito

This small hostel is very clean and comfortable, with Wi-Fi, breakfast, friendly, bi-lingual staff, nice, open common areas around a courtyard, and a shared kitchen. It's within walking distance to the Zocalo and main markets, and the hostel offers many tours through trusted tour operators and private parties not advertised anywhere else. Some excursions you can take include a trip to a Zapatista community, a workshop on how to make your own chocolate, among others.

Cost: 100 pesos for a bed in a shared dorm

Calle Tapachula #18
Barrio del Cerrio, San Cristobal de
las Casas
967-678-1741
psadaabuelito@live.com.mx
facebook.com/posadaabuelito

Hostel Qhia

This hostel is quiet and has a spacious common room on the second floor of the main building with a beautiful view of the mountains, complete with pillows and couches to lounge on. Hot water, clean rooms, shared kitchen, Wi-Fi and breakfast included. It's located a few blocks from the Santo Domingo crafts market on a quiet street. Staff is friendly and helpful, and the vibe is very relaxed.

Cost: 100 pesos for a bed in a shared dorm

Calle Tonala #5
Barrio del Cerrio, San Cristobal de
Las Casas
967-678-0594
qhiasancristobal@gmail.com
www.hostelqhia.com

Rossco Backpackers Hostel

This hostel has a great communal vibe, with bonfires every night, spacious indoor and outdoor seating, several dorm rooms to chose from, breakfast, shared kitchen, hot water, Wi-Fi, book exchange, friendly staff and tour information for guests. Located a few blocks from the Santo Domingo market.

Cost: 99 pesos for a bed in a shared dorm

Real de Mexicanos #16
Barrio del Cerrio, San Cristobal de
Las Casas
967-674-0525
contact@backpackerhostel.com.
mx
www.rosscohostel.com

Santo Domingo
This craft market is huge, and has anything you could ever want or need to buy in terms of indigenous and artisan goods. Jewelry, leather goods, woven tapestries, pillowcases, blankets and napkins, pottery, wooden textiles, bags, purses and clothing. Give yourself a few hours to explore the market in its entirety before you start buying.

The Mercado Municipal
This is where the locals come to shop for fruit, vegetables, meat, spices, chiles, raw food and even live chickens and roosters. It's packed with people and can be disorienting. Come with some patience and an open mind.

Mercado de Dulces y Artensanias
This is a small open-air market on the southern end of town. Inside, every kind of candy, cake and dessert they make in the region is sold, plus several stands with clothes, textiles, art, beaded and woven goods.

Along and around Real de Guadalupe are a variety of boutiques and stores that cater to both tourists and locals. Visit artisan markets before you make a purchase from a store, as you will most likely get a better deal buying directly from the source.

PALENQUE

With its lush jungle and spectacular ruins, Palenque draws tourists from around the world. Nearly 1,000 people visit the Palenque ruins daily, which are surrounded by waterfalls and thick greenery, howler monkeys and rare species of birds. Ancient Mayan tombs, buildings, and temples dating back to the 7th century are well-preserved and the intricate architecture is mind-boggling. Advanced aqueduct and drainage systems, multi-leveled buildings, burial sites and detailed adornments were constructed using basic tools to create this multifaceted city that still stands and fascinates visitors today.

Some people come to Palenque on guided day trips, while others choose to stay for a few days to explore the wildlife and thick forest that makes up the national park and surrounding areas. Don't want to stay in the city? El Panchan offers alternative lodging, nestled in the forest just outside the entrance to the park. While the modern city of Palenque is not nearly as striking or impressive as the ruins, it would be a great disservice to your trip to miss this ancient Mayan site.

HOW TO GET THERE

From San Cristobal
We're not sure why, but taking a tour to Palenque from San Cristobal de Las Casas is cheaper than taking a first class bus. You have some options when booking: you can either take the full tour to see the famous waterfalls of Agua Azul and Misol-Ha, ending the tour at the ruins in Palenque for a few hours before heading back to San Cristobal, or you can get dropped off in Palenque after seeing the waterfalls, stay the night in El Panchan and visit the ruins on your own the next day.

Taking a tour from San Cristobal is the best option, in our opinion, for a few reasons: first, you get to see waterfalls that are otherwise very difficult to get to on your own; second, it saves you money. We recommend staying the night in Palenque because doing the tour in its entirety means you'll have a very long day, getting picked up at 6 a.m. and returning to San Cristobal around 11 p.m., with limited time in the ruins.

The ride from San Cristobal to Palenque is about 6 hours. Check with the ADO bus ticketing office in San Cristobal for prices before booking a tour, in case the cost has dropped since we were there.

If you're heading to Palenque from other parts of Mexico, the easiest way to get there is to take the first class ADO bus. It will drop you off in the city center.

To get to El Panchan from the Palenque ADO bus station, cross the street and either take a private taxi, which should cost no more than 50 pesos, or wait for a shared colectivo van marked 'ruinas.' The shared ride costs 10 pesos.

STAY IN NEARBY EL PANCHAN

The city center of Palenque lacks charm, and there's not much to see or do there, other than eat. Instead, we recommend staying in El Panchan. Located at the entrance to the national park and ruins, this small section of the jungle has been turned into a quiet community of posadas, cabanas and restaurants surrounded by lush greenery, chirping birds, howler monkeys and other wildlife.

There are no ATMs, Internet, convenience stores or grocery stores in El Panchan. Take out money, buy water, snacks, fruit for breakfast and other necessities before you leave the city.

Don Muchos is the best restaurant in El Panchan, with a wide variety of food for breakfast, lunch and dinner. The restaurant is a popular hangout for travelers, and the bar gets busy at night. Food is reasonably priced and tasty.

El Panchan is very small. If none of the below accommodation options sound like what you're looking for, stop into the other posadas and cabanas along the way to see rooms and ask for rates.

THINGS TO KNOW

- It's hot and humid in Palenque. Make sure to drink a lot of water to stay hydrated.

- Bring bug spray, and apply it often. There are lots of bugs in the jungle, and they bite.

- You can hire an official guide once you get to the ruins, or just buy a ticket and explore them yourself. Guides can take you to out-of-the-way waterfalls and small ruins that are off the beaten path, and can explain the significance and history of each pre-Hispanic temple and building. Negotiate a price for the best deal, or join a group to cut down on the cost.

- It's best to get to the ruins as early as possible to avoid crowds and afternoon heat. You'll be most comfortable wearing shorts, walking shoes, a t-shirt and a hat. Bring a small backpack with bug spray, sunscreen, water, your camera and snacks.

- Entrance to the ruins is free for Mexican nationals on Sundays. It's very crowded on this day of the week.

- There are lots of vendors both inside and outside the ruins selling all sorts of textiles and handmade goods, but most artisan items sold in Palenque come from San Cristobal de Las Casas, meaning things are more expensive in Palenque. Wait to buy things in other parts of Chiapas if possible.

The road between Palenque and San Cristobal de Las Casas is dangerous to drive on at night. Day travel is the safest way to go between these two cities.

THINGS TO DO

National Park and Ruins

The ruins of Palenque are magnificent, well preserved and nestled in the jungle, making them dramatically different from the ruins of Chichen Itza. Walk through ancient Maya temples and buildings, and try to imagine what life was like here during the 7th century for the 8,000 people who inhabited the city. The main, central area you see is only one portion of the ruins that were discovered in the mid 1900s – the rest is hidden in the thick jungle around the main ruins site. An official guide can take you to see some of the more hidden ruins that you won't be able to find on your own. If you're exploring the park without a guide, after passing through the main entrance, visit the central ruins and continue downhill to see waterfalls and burial sites.

Cost: 27 pesos at the entrance to the national park; 57 pesos to enter the ruins.

Palenque Museum

Your entrance to the ruins includes a trip to the national park's museum, which is a short walk from the exit if you exited the park after passing by the waterfalls and burial site. Signs mark the way. The museum houses detailed historical information, a recreation of the Temple of Inscriptions (which is not open to visitors), jewelry and adornments found inside the ruins and tombs of royalty and high-ranking members of society, and explanations of architecture, calendars and symbols found throughout the site. They also include in-depth information on Mayan royalty, lineage and daily life for the common man.

Sunrise or Sunset Jungle Walking Tour

If you decide to stay in El Panchan and are interested in taking a guided walking tour to see howler monkeys, toucans, and other wildlife at sunrise or sunset, head to La Posada de Margarita and Ed and ask about rates and availability. This guided walking tour comes highly recommended from fellow travelers.

ACCOMMODATION

Posada de Margarita and Ed

This family-run posada in El Panchan is quiet and clean. Beds are comfortable and hot water is on 24-hours. Be advised that reception closes during the early evening and they have a strict check-out policy. The most basic cabanas have a fan, hot water and a double bed; rooms in the main area of the posada have air conditioning and televisions.

To get there, enter El Panchan, walk past Don Muchos and continue on the main road. Posada de Margarita and Ed will be on your right, where the road ends. Reception is past the first set of cabanas upstairs in the main house.

Cost: 250 pesos for a basic cabana. 400 pesos for a room with air conditioning and TV.

Jungle Palace

The most economical rooms here have a shared bathroom for guests; more expensive rooms come with a private bathroom. There is a travel desk out front offering guided tours to ruins and nearby waterfalls. Be advised that this posada does not have air conditioning.

Located directly across from Posada de Margarita and Ed. Talk to staff stationed at the tour guide stand for availability.

Cost: 100 pesos for a private room with a shared bath; 200 pesos for a room with private bath.

Posada de Los Angeles

If you're pressed for time and want to stay in the center, this posada is an acceptable option. It's located right across the street from the ADO bus station and OXXO. Staff is friendly and helpful, though not bilingual. Private rooms are basic and clean, with a fan and double beds.

Located directly across the street from the ADO bus station and OXXO in the city center of Palenque.

Cost: 120 pesos for a basic, private room

There are vendors selling wares in the ruins in Palenque, but everything seems to come from San Cristobal de las Casas, and is more expensive here. If you see something you must have, buy it—but be aware that you might find what you're looking for at a better rate in San Cristobal.

YUCATAN and QUINTANA ROO

Welcome to the Yucatan and Quintana Roo, where the people are as warm as the weather. The white sand beaches here are among the most beautiful in the world, and there's plenty of opportunity for you to soak up the sun, learn a new water sport, or go out on the town. While Cancun is spring break year-round, neighboring beach towns still have a small-town feel. Interested in ruins? Chichen Itza has some of the largest and most visited ruins in the country.

TOP ⭐ PICKS

Best pre-Hispanic dish:
Cochinita Pibil in Merida

Best white sand beach:
Tulum

Best Trip Off The Beaten Path:
The Biosphere of Sian Ka'an

YUCATAN PENINSULA

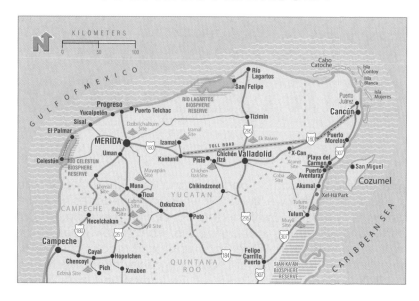

MERIDA & YUCATAN STATE

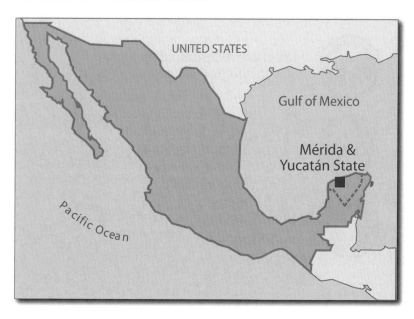

MERIDA & YUCATAN STATE

1	Municipal Market	5	Plaza Mayor	9	Parque Hidalgo
2	García Rejón Market	6.	Cathedral	10	Teatro Peón Contreras
3	Casa de Montejo	7	Mérida Museum	11	Palacio Cantón
4	Palacio Municipal	8.	Palacio de Gobierno	12	MACAY Museum
				13	University of Yucatán

MERIDA

O Merida, how your people love thee. The capital city of the Yucatan is full of pre-Hispanic culture, history, museums, markets and charm. Locals are eager to talk and help out a single girl on the road and you're likely to get stopped at least once for a friendly chat in the Zocalo. Don't be put off by this—Merida is just as interested in your story as you are in hers.

The shopping here is the best in the region, and the most sought after item is the hammock. Don't be fooled; not all hammocks are created equal. The production of these woven creations is intricate and time consuming, and the end result is one of the best naps you've ever had. They're sold practically everywhere, along with jewelry, textiles, clothes and art.

Pre-Hispanic restaurants line streets and are filled with smells and traditions of Mexico's indigenous past (and present). *Cochinita Pibil*, a meat dish full of flavor and topped with a magic sauce, is the local favorite. Dive in with an open mind and a hearty appetite for all things Yucatan and you're sure to come out of Merida with a few new friends.

HOW TO GET THERE

Merida's airport has flights arriving daily from domestic and international destinations:

Airport Code: MID

Carretera Merida a Uman
Km 14.5
Merida, Yucatan
www.asur.com.mx

CAME is the first class bus station, and is located on 69 street, between 70 and 71 street. Major bus lines at this station are ADO, GL and UNO.

THINGS TO KNOW

- The city is set up on a grid. Odd numbers run east/west; even numbers run north/south.

- You will most likely walk everywhere, so be sure to wear the right shoes. At night, things really die down here.

- The cultural center of the city is the Zocalo. It is the central square.

- There are several types of hammocks available for purchase. We were advised to ask for the "*hammaca local*," or local hammock, as it is the most sturdy. We also heard it's the best bang for your buck.

- Save space in your backpack and money for Merida – shopping is big here, and lots of goods are handmade of excellent quality.

- Eat at a pre-Hispanic restaurant. Order cochinita pibil. Thank us later.

- Sunday is the best day of the week to be in Merida. The Zocalo is closed off to cars and is full of people and vendors selling all things Yucatan. Locals spend the day with friends and family, dining in restaurants and enjoying the city.

- Pick up a *Yucatan Today* at the tourism information office. It has all sorts of useful information, local events and happenings. *www.yucatantoday.com*

Zocalo

The center of downtown Merida is the Zocalo. There are numerous shady benches and chairs to take a seat, listen to the birds chirp and people watch. It's a great spot to take a break from walking around in the heat. Stop by on Sunday for some shopping – street vendors set up weekly.

Cathedral *"La iglesia tiene la necesidad de arte"*

This cathedral is a work of art, dating back to the 16th century, and it houses one of the largest crucifixes we've ever seen. It's beautiful and striking. Be sure to keep your voice down once inside for those who are there for worship. Feel free to take photos.

Palacio Municipal

This palace is beautiful inside, but you'll need to buy a ticket to an event to see it. Exhibition listings and information are posted curbside out front.

MACAY

Merida's Contemporary Art Museum houses permanent and rotating exhibits, and is innovating and interesting. It's also free seven days a week! If you bring a large bag, you'll have to check it at the front desk. Our favorite exhibit there was one that showcased individual working girls of Merida, called "Las Mujeres del 58." Profiles and photos told hard stories of why each woman works on the street, selling her body for what she can. For most it came out of necessity.

Palacio del Gobierno

Inside this mint government building are murals by Salvador Alvarado, depicting the conquering of the Yucatan and Mayan people by the Spanish. His art is hung within the Palacio's arches. Murals illustrate Mexico's struggle and liberation. There is also a tourism information office located at the entrance.

Anthropology Museum

If you're interested in the Mayan and other pre-Hispanic cultures, this museum is perfect for you. Inside is specific information on numerology, astrology, trading, the Mayan calendar, history and other beliefs of the Mayan people. Also on display are pottery, paintings, jewelry and textiles. Upstairs is an exhibit dedicated to the first governor of the Yucatan who lived in the old colonial building with his family.

Cost: 47 pesos

Museo de la Ciudad

Merida's city museum is free and a good place to learn about the city's history. Information is provided in both English and Spanish.

Walk Down Calle 60

Take a walk from the Zocalo towards the Anthropology Museum on Calle 60 and you'll run into the University of the Yucatan, Parque de Santa Lucia and theater, the Parque de la Madre, Peon Contreras Theater, other small parks and plazas. This is a great walk to take photos, and there are many places available along the way to have a seat and take a break.

Cenotes

There are several *cenotes*, or natural sinkholes, located around Merida. Ask your hostel staff for details on how to get there.

ACCOMMODATION

Hostel Nomadas

This hostel has a pool and shaded garden area, which is great for hot afternoons after sightseeing is through. There is Wi-Fi, individual guest hammocks in rooms, continental breakfast, large lockers and a great communal feel – the hostel can hold up to 100 people. Very popular with backpackers. They also offer free salsa lessons Monday through Friday, have a travel desk at your disposal and offer tours to nearby points of interest.

Cost: 129 pesos for a bed in a mixed dorm

Calle 62 #433;
Cross Street is Calle 51
Centro, Merida, Yucatan
+52 999-924-5223
www.nomadastravel.com

Hostel Zocalo

Located on the main square, this old colonial house was converted into a hostel, and arguably has the best location of all accommodations in Merida. Some of the rooms have balconies overlooking the plaza, which is great for people watching and taking in views of the city. Huge continental breakfast, Wi-Fi, shared kitchen, 24-hour reception and security, and many return customers! Note: It can be somewhat loud here at night in rooms with balconies. Bring earplugs.

Cost: 85–100 pesos for a bed in a mixed dorm

Calle 63 #508,
between Calles 62 and 60
Centro, Merida, Yucatan
+52 999-930-9562

La Casa de Tio Rafa

If you're into a more intimate setting, this hostel is for you. With a maximum capacity of 15 with two dorm rooms and a private suite, this hostel is quaint and relaxing. Pool, rooftop terrace, continental breakfast, shared kitchen and laundry facilities available. Friendly bilingual staff are happy to help backpackers with tour ideas and things to do on your own without the need of a guide.

Cost: 100 pesos for a bed in a shared dorm

Calle 65 #589,
between Calles 72 and 74
Centro, Merida, Yucatan
+52 999-924-9446
www.lacasadeltiorafa.com

SHOPPING

Casa de las Artensanias
A little bit of everything can be found in this market. It's located on Calle 63, between 64 and 66.

Mundo Maya
Located right by the Zocalo on Calle 61 and Calle 62, this shop has a wide range of jewelry, stones, hammocks, clothes and very friendly and helpful owners. Staff is there creating hand-made woven items.

Street Boutiques
They're everywhere. Stop in, browse, buy.

Lucas de Galvez Market
The main downtown market is huge and sells everything you could

imagine. Make sure to ask before taking photos of vendors and what they're selling. Calle 60 and 65.

Sunday at the Zocalo
The Zocalo is closed to cars on Sundays, and street vendors set up throughout the plaza. It's a great place and time to browse, take photos and buy a few items.

You'll stumble upon other smaller markets throughout your stay in Merida. People come from far and wide to sell their unique arts, crafts, clothes and textiles to tourists and locals alike. Happy hunting!

CHICHEN ITZA

Chichen Itza is one of the 7 wonders of the world, a UNESCO World Heritage Site, and one of the most famous Mayan archeological sites in the region. It's a popular daytrip from nearby Cancun or Merida and one that should not be missed.

HOW TO GET THERE

Buses from every major town and city in the Yucatan and Quintana Roo go to Chichen Itza daily. Buy your bus ticket to and away from Chichen Itza before you go. Many people choose to go to the ruins from the coast, and then continue on to Merida, or stay in the town of Piste, 2 km. away, the night before they visit the ruins.

THINGS TO KNOW

- There are no hostels in Chichen Itza. ADO and other bus companies drop you off directly outside of the ruins entrance, and pick you up in the same spot.

- Give yourself 3 hours to see the site in its entirety, give or take. Plan your transportation accordingly.

- As a foreigner, you'll need to buy two tickets at two separate windows before you're allowed to enter the ruins. One is a state ticket fee, and the other is federal. Tickets are 57 and 120 pesos, for a total of 177 pesos to enter.

- It's hot! Loose fitting clothes are most comfortable, with sneakers or hiking shoes, a hat and lots of sunscreen. The earlier you can get there the better – early means less people and less heat. If early is not an option, shoot for 2 p.m. or later, when the sun's peak hours are over.

- Ask for a map (they are available at the first ticket stand) and explore the ruins by yourself, or hire an English-speaking guide for 600 pesos for the day. Representatives may also be able to set you up with a group of people if you're solo to cut down on cost.

If you're stopping at Chichen Itza between cities, where do you leave your stuff?

They offer a free bag check at the entrance, but we noticed that the room does not have the tightest security. For the record, we didn't have any problems with theft, but to be safe, carry the things you can't part with on you – passport, credit cards, cash, laptop, etc.

What else should you bring?

Water, lunch or snacks, bug spray, sunscreen, hat, camera, pesos. There are cafes and restaurants located at the entrance and inside the ruins, but they are expensive. Load up on what you'll want to eat and drink before you go. You also might want to do some shopping – there are literally hundreds of vendors set up inside, selling handcrafts, clothes, jewelry, toys, and other goods. Feel free to negotiate prices. A small backpack is the best for carrying your stuff around the site.

IT GETS CROWDED...

On Sundays, when it's free for Mexican national citizens to visit Chichen Itza. Take this into consideration when deciding what day to go. It's also extremely crowded during the spring equinox, which attracts visitors from all over the world. The shadow of a serpent appears at sunrise and sunset through intricate patterns carved into the great buildings, and is a sign of how important astronomy and the calendar was to the Mayans.

Equinox date: March 21. *** We also heard that it's possible to see the serpent two days before and after the 21st of March. ***

CANCUN

Monday, party. Tuesday, party. Wednesday, party. Thursday, more party. As they say in Mexico, Cancun is *pura fiesta*. This place is spring break year round, catering to tourists from all over the world who come here for a good time, and not for a long time. The turnover is pretty incredible, topping off somewhere in the millions, especially in high season (about November through April). The weather's warm, the beaches are gorgeous, and there are tours for just about anything you'd like to do, as long as you have enough money to pay for it.

This area of Mexico is newly developed, all things considered. A plan was devised and implemented in the 70's to turn this practically desolate strip of pristine beaches and lush jungle into a vacation destination. Hotels, all-inclusive resorts, clubs, store-fronts and golf-courses were built in what is now known as the hotel zone, and permanent residences, hospitals and schools were constructed in the center of town. Throw in an international airport, roads connecting to other parts of mainland Mexico, and you've got a fully functioning vacation hub for people from around the world.

Cancun is big on the backpacker circuit, so staying a few days won't break the bank. Almost every hostel is located in the center of town, which is an easy bus ride to the beach and hotel zone. Cancun is a good place to start your trip of the Yucatan and Quintana Roo if you plan to visit; just don't be surprised if you're hungover at least once by the time you leave.

HOW TO GET THERE

Cancun's international airport (CUN) has daily flights arriving from almost every major city in the world.

Airport Code: CUN

If you're flying into Cancun, avoid taking a taxi to your accommodation, as it can cost anywhere from 300–500 pesos for a ride. The ADO bus heads straight to the central bus station multiple times a day for much cheaper (52 pesos), and almost every hostel is within walking distance of the bus station. Bus company ticket booths are directly outside the main terminal. Once outside the airport, turn right, and look for ADO.

If you're staying in the center of the city, you'll need to take a bus to get to the beach and hotel zone. The R-1 bus goes direct along Tulum Avenue, and costs 8.5 pesos.

THINGS TO KNOW

• Everything is more expensive in the hotel zone. Do your shopping in the center of town to save money.

• Accommodation prices fluctuate depending the season. Costs are highest during spring break (March), Semana Santa (April), Christmas and New Year's Eve.

• The beaches in this area of the country are stunning – white, cool sand, warm waves and some of the most beautiful blue and green water in the world. Do your part in keeping it clean and pick up your trash.

• Currents can be strong. Make sure to check the flags along the beach before going in. Red means currents are extremely powerful. Walk to where you see a yellow flag to be safe.

- All Mexican beaches are public property. You are welcome to visit any of them, even if a big resort occupies the space directly behind it. Each beach has a public entrance from the street.

- All hostels offer organized tours, but you may be able to find a cheaper price from off the street. People walk around selling tours all day, and stay stationed along the beach and Tulum Avenue.

For cheap street food in the center, head to Parque de las Palapas.

PARTY, PARTY, PARTY

Before you go out and hit the town, keep these things in mind:

- Most club entrance fees are expensive; the larger ones more so. Wristbands can cost anywhere from 200–600 pesos, and include an open bar. Make sure to monitor how much alcohol you take in, and to drink lots of water.

- The typical young tourist here is one who drinks all night, dances on the bar and is easily seduced. By all means, enjoy yourself, but don't do anything you'll regret in the morning! Only you can decide what that means.

- Most people dress up for nights on the town. This includes high heels, mini-skirts, mini-dresses… pretty much mini everything. We're not suggesting you dress this way; it's just something to be aware of.

- Planning to head out to a club in the hotel zone? Pay your entrance fee at the door rather than buying it from a vendor on the street - most of the time, the scalper rates are more expensive. They'll tell you they'll walk you straight in, and can be quite persuasive, but club lines move quickly.

SIGHTS

Beaches
There are 10 major beaches in Cancun, and all are impressive. Our favorite is Chac Mool.

Day Trips

Every hostel offers group day trips to nearby ruins, smaller beach towns and eco parks. Trips include stops in Playa del Carmen, Isla de las Mujeres, Tulum, Chichen Itza, cenotes and more. All of these places can be visited independently, but if you want to do an organized tour, they are here for you. Prices vary depending on duration, destinations and activities.

Water Sports

Snorkel, jet ski, stand-up paddleboard, parasail, sailboard. You can rent equipment or pay for a lesson along the beach.

Isla De Las Mujeres

This nearby island can be visited daily via ferry. Snorkeling is a popular activity here, and it's a nice break from the madness of Cancun.

ACCOMMODATION

Mundo Joven Hostel

This large hostel has four floors, a rooftop terrace, bar and Jacuzzi, and is a great place to meet fellow travelers. Wi-Fi throughout means you can lay in bed and Skype. Staff is bilingual and very helpful. The female-only dorm has air conditioning and private bathrooms. Breakfast included.

Cost: 200 pesos for a shared dorm

Uxmal 25
Colonial Centro, Cancun,
Quintana Roo
998-898-2104
www.mundojovenhostels.com

Quetzal Hostel

This hostel is like an old house, and the open vibe keeps people coming back. There is a party manager for organized events, large garden spaces with hammocks, a rooftop terrace and lots of common space. Payment for a bed in a mixed dorm includes breakfast and dinner; a local chef prepares the latter.

Cost: 220 pesos for a bed in a mixed dorm

Orquideas N 10
Colonial Centro, Cancun,
Quintana Roo
998-883-9821
www.quetzal-hostel.com

Ka'beh Cancun Hostel

The owner of this hostel believes in slow travel, so there is no check-in or check out time, and you're welcome to leave your bags for long-term storage if you plan to come back to Cancun. Custom made bunk beds mean you can sit all the way up without hitting your head, and the lockers are huge. Fancy a nice, long soak instead of a shower? There's a bathtub! Breakfast included. Dependable Wi-Fi. Ask about work options if you're short on cash.

Cost: 150 pesos for a bed in a shared dorm

Alcatraces 45
Colonial Centro, Cancun,
Quintana Roo
998-892-7902

Mayan Hostel
This hostel has somewhat of a relaxed, rasta vibe. Breakfast is included and the menu changes daily, with a few staple items, like beans, tortillas and coffee. The manager, Marcus, is very knowledgeable about the Yucatan peninsula, and you'd be wise to pick his brain on where to go if you're looking to get off the backpacker trail. Ask for work options if you're looking

to stay a while. Rooftop terrace, front patio, great location.

Cost: 140 pesos for a room in a shared dorm

Margaritas 17
Colonial Centro, Cancun,
Quintana Roo
998-140-5253

Hostel Mayapan
If you're dying to stay in the hotel zone, this is pretty much the only budget option. Located in a strip mall, it's a 5-minute walk to the beach and clubs. 24-hour reception, but lockers are tiny. Common areas are somewhat lacking, but there are 20 beds in the shared dorm, so it's probable that you'll meet a few people to spend the day with.

Cost: 220 pesos for a bed in a shared dorm

Boulevard Kukulkan Km. 8.5
Shopping Center Mayfair,
Downstairs
Hotel Zone, Cancun, Quintana Roo
998-883-3227
www.hostelmayapan.com

SHOPPING

Shops are located along every street in the hotel zone, offering the standard clothes and crafts, but you're most likely to get a better deal on the same items in the center of town.

Mercado 28
Large, open-air market in the center of town full of the standard

Mexican fare – purses, sarongs, clothes, art and jewelry. Vendors can be somewhat pushy since the market is mainly for tourists. Feel free to barter. Open daily.

Mercado 23
Also located in the center of town, this is where the locals shop. Fruits, vegetables, meat, dried goods, spices and other raw goods can be purchased here. There's also a ready-made food section. A good place to have lunch and take photos. Open daily.

PLAYA DEL CARMEN

If Cancun had a younger sister, it would be Playa del Carmen – not nearly as big, not quite as old, but the family resemblance is unmistakable. Born a little later out of the same idea, Playa is another place that is known for its beautiful beaches and up-all-night life, making it a popular destination for English-speaking and other foreign tourists. But there is one major difference between it and Cancun: the size. Playa del Carmen is easy to navigate and completely walkable, and is much more quaint than its northern counterpart.

The beaches in Playa are more relaxed than those in Cancun – thumping club music is replaced with live bands, reggae and in some cases, nothing at all except the sound of the ocean. The water is warm and crystal clear, the sunsets are beautiful, and the vibe is laid back. It's in these quiet moments that you can imagine what the quiet village was like years ago, before plans were made to turn it into what it is today. Water sports are readily available if you feel the urge to get active – snorkel, dive, parasail, kite surf, fish, jet ski, etc., and Cozumel just a short ferry ride away.

Fifth Avenue is the heart of downtown. It's a busy walk-street full of people, tour guides and companies, shops, boutiques, hotels, restaurants, art galleries, spas, street artists, cafes (there's even a Starbucks), and the clubs are right around the corner. Playa del Carmen is a place to treat yourself to a nice dinner, put up your feet and relax, until it's time to go out again, of course.

You don't need more than a few days to see Playa del Carmen, but many people come and want to stay. It's somewhere in between Cancun and Tulum in terms of vibe and intensity (Cancun being crazy party time, Tulum quiet and calm), and the living's easy by the beach. Enjoy!

HOW TO GET THERE

Playa del Carmen's main bus station is located on 5th Avenue, between Juarez Avenue and 2nd Avenue. Buses run frequently from Cancun. The ride is about an hour on a first class bus. Cost is 48 pesos.

The city is easily navigated, and runs on a grid. All streets are numerical. Fifth Avenue is the main street that runs north/south through town.

THINGS TO KNOW

- New hotels, hostels and other accommodation options pop up all the time, and rates are seasonal. Expect to pay more during December and April.

- For cheaper eats, head east, away from the beach and the busy tourist section of town.

- Temperatures are hot and humid, even at night. Staying in a hostel with air conditioning is preferable, and you'll be glad you did. Waking up sweaty is never fun.

- Clubs are located where 5th Avenue meets 12th Avenue. Some clubs will charge an entrance fee to get in and have a separate rate for an open bar. The difference in these rates is usually substantial. If the club looks packed, it will probably be hard to get a drink. In that case, pay the entrance fee only and buy drinks one at a time. You'll save money.

- Most of what you'll want to do is in downtown – the bus station, hostels, nightlife, restaurants, shops and bars are all located in this area.

- Wear bug spray. All the time. Mosquitos love tourist skin.

SIGHTS

Cozumel
This famous island known for its offshore reefs, snorkeling and diving is off the coast of Playa del Carmen, and is a great day trip. The ferry leaves from the pier located next to Señor Frogs nearly every hour and takes about 45 minutes. Cost is 155 pesos for adults. For more information, visit *www.mexicowaterjets.com*.

Beaches
All of the hostels listed in this chapter are walking distance from miles of beautiful beaches. Bring sunscreen, a hat, towel and other beach gear.

Party
Playa del Carmen comes alive at night. Fifth Avenue is bustling with people after the sun goes down and bars and clubs are packed by midnight. There's a mix of live music, laid back lounges, sports bars and dance clubs. Pick your poison and mingle – when we were there, the people were friendly and open.

Water Sports
Snorkel, parasail, Jet Ski, kite surf, swim, dive, etc. Stations are set up along the beach with people who can rent you equipment and provide lessons if needed. Shop around for the best deal.

Cenotes

Underwater caves are prevalent in this area of the country, as they are in Tulum. You'll need a guide to take you, which won't be hard to find. Ask your hostel staff, tour companies on the beach and 5th Avenue for details.

Tours

They're everywhere, and can take you wherever you want to go. Cozumel, transport to and from Chichen Itza, Tulum, Akumal, the cenotes and everything in between. If you plan to hit these spots on your own, you won't be in need of a tour. If you're short on time, you may want to consider taking a day trip or two to nearby points of interest.

ACCOMMODATION

Hostel 3B

This hostel is really modern and fancy, by hostel standards— white and black décor, comfy beds, big lockers and there is air-conditioning in every room. Their motto is cheap and chic, and it shows. Located two blocks from the bus station and three blocks from the beach, they have a small shared kitchen, Wi-Fi and friendly staff. Breakfast not included but is available for an additional fee.

Cost: 160–180 pesos for a bed in a shared dorm

10th Avenue and 1st Avenue South
Playa del Carmen, Quintana Roo
984-147-1207
info@hostel3b.com
www.hostel3b.com

Hostel Rio Playa

Really friendly, bilingual front desk staff. Bathrooms are inside

all rooms, and they have a rooftop pool and bar, where there's a ladies night once a week. Really popular with back-packers and is a great place to meet people. It fills up during high season, so call in advance to reserve a bed. Wi-Fi, breakfast included, air-condi-tioning, and tours available. Located one block from the beach.

Cost: 150 pesos for a bed in a shared dorm

Calle 8 between 5th Avenue and 10th Avenue
Playa del Carmen, Quintana Roo
984-127-0594

Hostel Che

The various dorms in this hostel are all mixed, and bath-rooms are inside the dorms. Friendly, bilingual staff is very accommodating. The rooftop bar hosts events, including 2 for 1 nights. Shared kitchen, young vibe, air-conditioning, and some of the rooms have spacious balconies. Walking distance to the beach and bus station.

Cost: 120-180 pesos for a bed in a shared dorm

Calle 6 between 15th and 20th Avenue
Playa del Carmen, Quintana Roo
984-147-1741
hostelche@gmail.com
www.hostelche.com.mx

SHOPPING

Fifth Avenue
This is the place to go for shopping in Playa. While some of the stores are quite upscale, others are more like a one-stop outlet for cheap souvenirs. Fifth Avenue is long and busy, and some of the big stores offer the same goods. Walk around for the best deal.

COSTA MAYA REGION

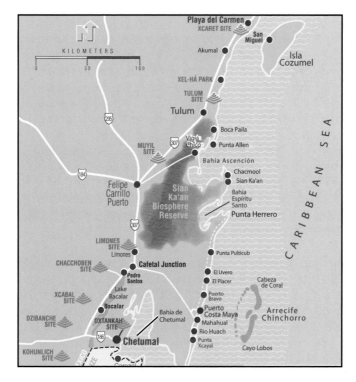

TULUM

About an hour south of Playa del Carmen is Tulum, a considerably quieter beach community with a very laid-back personality. This place reminds us of what Cancun and Playa del Carmen were before they expanded into serious tourist destinations. Don't get us wrong – Tulum is still touristy, but it's not the place to go if you're looking for big clubs, thumping techno and in-your-face tour guides looking to sell you a day trip; quite the opposite actually.

Tulum is the kind of place where you rent a bike for a day, ride to the ruins that the Mayans left right on the beach, lay in the sun or a hammock, go for a swim in the ocean, eat delicious seafood and relax. There aren't big buses for public transportation, but smaller vans, called colectivos, that can get you wherever you want to go, and most of the hostels have a serious communal feel. This is a great place to slow down and take a breather, if you have the luxury to do so.

Several cenotes in the area are good for both snorkeling and diving, and if you fancy a swim with sea turtles and ocean wildlife, there's a beach for that too. Looking for something to do that's really off the beaten path? The bioreserve of Sian Ka'an is a 30-minute drive from town, and even though you'll need a guide to take you inside, once there, your group will be the only people for as far as the eye can see.

HOW TO GET THERE

ADO, UNO and Mayab are the major bus companies that go to Tulum. Trips are very frequent from Playa del Carmen, Cancun, Merida, and just about anywhere else in the Yucatan and Quintana Roo.

The bus station is located in downtown, on the main road called Tulum Street or Avenue, depending on whom you ask. The hostels we recommend in this chapter are all a short walk from the bus station. Tulum is pretty small, as you will soon find out!

THINGS TO KNOW

• The ruins in Tulum are the only major Mayan ruins that are located on the ocean. This makes for great photo ops, and you can also kill two birds with one stone – head to the ruins, and when you're done checking them out, walk down the back stairs for a beach day.

• Renting a bike for a day should cost you around 80 pesos.

• Colectivos are the basic form of public transportation and 15 pesos will get you anywhere you want to go in town.

• Most of the hostels and budget accommodations are located downtown, meaning you will need to rent a bike or take a colectivo to get to the beach.

• If you are certified to dive, there are several cenotes and beaches that are of interest. The best cenotes for snorkeling are Dos Ojos and the Gran Cenote. You can go by yourself, but it's dark in there! Make sure to have good snorkel equipment, a strong underwater flashlight and a life jacket. You can also go with a guide who will provide all of this equipment and lead you through the cave. Ask your hostel staff for guided tour options.

• Visit Sian Ka'an! It's worth it! Check out the 'Things To Do' section for contact information.

• If you're sick of meat at this point, there are many vegetarian restaurant options in Tulum – ask your hostel staff for recommendations.

Cenotes
There are many cenotes in Tulum and neighboring areas, and swimming in these freshwater caves is an incredible experience. The Mayans used them for sacrifices and rituals, and for that reason (among others), they are considered sacred. Many of them connect through underground tunnels. Pretty cool!

Snorkel
Fun and easy, this is a great way to check out coral reefs, ocean wildlife and cenotes. You can rent snorkel equipment just about anywhere, or go on a tour of the area and equipment will be provided for you.

Dive
If you're certified to dive, Tulum is a great place to do it! Many people come here specifically to dive in cenotes.

Mayan Ruins
The Mayan ruins of Tulum are the only ruins that are located on the beach. It's best to go at the beginning or the end of the day – weather is hot and it gets pretty crowded. Bring a bathing suit, beach gear and camera – you can walk down stairs to the beach after you're done exploring the ruins. Entrance is 57 pesos.

Beach
The beaches in Tulum are gorgeous – cold, white sand, crystal clear turquoise water and plenty of space to sprawl out.

Akumal
This beach is about halfway between Playa del Carmen and Tulum. Head here to swim with sea turtles and other ocean wildlife, and check out some coral reefs. If you can get your hands on an underwater camera, you'll get some great photos!

Sian Ka'an Biosphere Reserve
This biosphere is the largest protected area in the Mexican Caribbean, and is part of the UNESCO's Man and Biosphere program and is a World Heritage Site. There are over 100 different kinds of mammals on site, beautiful beaches, wetlands and walking trails. Tours of the area include snorkeling and kayaking at sunrise or sunset. To set up a tour or get more information, email *greenbirdtours@hotmail.com*.

ACCOMMODATION

The Weary Traveler Hostel

This place has a serious communal feel, right down to the food. They have a "burn your own meat" philosophy – essentially, you buy your meat or fish from the kitchen and cook it yourself. This also applies to the included breakfast. What we like most about this place is the FREE daily beach transportation, free water, hammocks for lounging and "pay at the end" policy – you can charge everything you want and pay at checkout. Super convenient.

From the bus station, walk outside the bus station and turn right. The Weary Traveler is about 3 blocks down the road.

Cost: 150 pesos for a dorm in a shared room

Tulum 36
77780 Tulum, Quintana Roo
984-871-2390
reservations@wearytravelerhostel.com
www.wearytravelerhostel.com

Casa Del Sol Hostel

Comfortable and centrally located, this hostel has basic accommodation, a rooftop terrace, free breakfast, vegetarian options, hammocks, a shared kitchen and 24-hour reception. It's a short walk from the bus station and the staff is very friendly and knowledgeable.

From the bus station, walk outside the bus station and turn right. Follow signs for Casa Del Sol Hostel.

Cost: 150–190 pesos

815 Polar Pte.
77780, Tulum, Quintana Roo
984-129-6424
www.casadelsolhostels.com

SHOPPING

There are some boutiques and an artisan market located on the road to the Mayan ruins, but we recommend saving your shopping for Merida and Chichen Itza, if you plan to go there. Prices are less expensive and there is a much larger quantity of goods to choose from.

Isla de Las Mujeres

Take a trip to this little white sand island off of Cancun to have a few quiet days lounging in the sun, snorkeling or diving. The island is beautiful and a nice break from the big city resort life, and is easy to go to – you can take a ferry from either ferry dock in Cancun, Puerto Juarez or Gran Puerto Cancun, about 15 minutes north of downtown. The ride takes about 20 minutes, and should cost about 80 pesos.

Hotel El Caracol
We heard great things about this hotel. Rates are reasonable, rooms are very clean, and Hugo, the owner, is very helpful and friendly. For what you would pay to stay at a hostel on the island (and we heard several have bed bugs) you get a whole room to yourself at this place. Not bad, right?

Cost: 250–350 pesos for a private room with a fan.

Av. Matamoros #5
Isla Mujeres, Quintana Roo
huguin_pro@yahoo.com
Isla-mujeres.net/hotelcaracol

For more information on the island, places to stay and things to do, check out www.isla-mujeres.net.

COZUMEL

The island of Cozumel is a short ferry ride from Playa del Carmen, and can also be accessed via plane from Cancun. The island is very popular among divers, and while it's starting to become very popular for tourists, it still hasn't exploded like nearby Cancun.

HOW TO GET THERE

Boat
The ferry leaves from Playa Del Carmen every hour and costs 156 pesos. Buy a one-way ticket because there are a couple of different companies that leave the dock and the tickets are non-transferable.

To arrive from Cancun, take the bus from Cancun to Playa del Carmen, or fly. Flights leave Cancun's domestic terminal and cost about USD $75.

THINGS TO KNOW

- Diving is popular in Cozumel and there are several dive shops throughout the main drag. If you're experienced, shop around to see if there are any differences in price.

- San Miguel is the main town on the island. It is located on the west side of the island, where most of the development is.

- The east side of the island is still largely undeveloped and the beaches are beautiful. Be aware though, currents and under-tows on this side of the island make it dangerous for swimming.

THINGS TO DO

San Gervasio Mayan Ruins
Take a visit to the San Gervasio ruins, where Mayan women used to make pilgrimage at least once in their lives. The park is also a wildlife refuge and home to some local iguanas. Entrance is 77 pesos.

Diving

There are several dive shops in Cozumel. If you don't know how to dive, most will offer a course before they take you out. It costs around $70 USD for a dive session, and you'll also have to pay for equipment and a marine park fee.

Snorkeling

Diving not your thing? You'll be able to find several companies offering snorkeling trips. There are also several tours on boats with glass-bottoms that make enjoying the ocean life a breeze.

ACCOMMODATION

Beachouse Hostel

This popular hostel is located just 3km outside of the center of town, and has a private beach, a dive shop and diving lessons. The private rooms are large and clean, and the communal kitchen is open for you to use. Free coffee, purified water, web access and Wi-Fi. Taxi from downtown costs 80–100 pesos, and they can arrange scooter rental if you ask in advance. It's wise to book ahead as they have only 7 rooms.

Cost: 355–500 pesos

Beachouse Hostel Cozumel (located next to the golf club) Country Club Estate / Lote 36 77600 Cozumel 987-872-6285 987-107-6744 (cell) beachousecozumel@gmail.com www.cozumel.net/bb/beachouse-cozumel

Tamarindo Cozumel

For private rooms in the heart of San Miguel, Tamarindo Cozumel is a great option. This bed and breakfast has only four cozy rooms, plus a thatched-roof bungalow, so call or visit their website ahead of time to be sure you get a spot! It's 10 minutes away from the pier if you walk, or $4 USD for a taxi.

Cost: 200–350 pesos

Once you arrive at the pier, make a left and walk along the ocean-front. On the second street, make a right, this is Calle 4 Norte where Tamarindo is lcoated. Walk four blocks and you will see Tamarindo on the left handside of the street. That will take 10 minutes.

Calle 4 Norte #421, entre 20 y 25 Ave 987-872-6190 or 987-872-3614 www.tamarindobedandbreakfast. com

SHOPPING

You can buy lots of goodies in Cozumel, but much of what you see will be touristy and likely more expensive than other parts of Mexico. Cozumel is know for their affordable silver, however. Just make sure you see a stamp that says ".925" before you buy.

VOLUNTEERING IN MEXICO

VOLUNTEERING

Volunteering is a wonderful way to get to know a culture from the inside-out and make some true and lasting friendships. Unfortunately, many third-party companies that promise amazing and exotic volunteer experiences also cost thousands of dollars— and fall well short of the promises they make on their websites.

We don't think that volunteering should cost you anything aside from basic costs to cover food and accommodation, and there are several local organizations in Mexico that share that belief.

From working in an orphanage to helping save sea turtles, this list of organizations has a little bit of something for everyone. Contact these organizations yourself to see how you can help—you'll be glad you did.

Guadalajara Learning Center

The GLC is a Spanish learning center that works with MAMA, the Movement to Support Abandoned Minors, that is dedicated to defending, protecting, and improving the lives of homeless, abandoned and abused children who live and work on the street. They fulfill this mission with a number of programs that provide education and nourishment. Volunteers are needed to support these programs and build relationships with the children.

Minimum Requirement: 3 weeks
Cost: Volunteering is free, but language classes from GLC are not.
Based Out Of: Guadalajara

Tel Int.: + 011 52 333-635-2535
Tel from Mexico: 01 333-635-2535
Toll free # USA: 1-866-275-5222
Toll free # Canada: 1-877-240-9736
glc@glc.com.mx
www.glc.com.mx

Oaxaca Streetchildren Grassroots

More than 3 million people in Oaxaca live in extreme poverty and many families survive on just a few dollars a day. Because of this, many children work and live on the street, trying to make ends meet. Oaxaca Streetchildren Grassroots is a non-profit organization that aims to end the cycle of poverty and allow children a chance at a promising future. Volunteers are needed to assist in the kitchen, library and office and to work with the children, either short-term or long-term.

Minimum Requirement: None, but longer stays are encouraged.
Cost: Free
Based Out Of: Oaxaca

Mexico Phone: 501-1069
From the USA: +011 52 951-501-1069
www.oaxacastreetchildrengrassroots.org

Casa de Los Angeles

Located in the heart of San Miguel de Allende, Casa de Los Angeles provides day care programs for children whose parents travel into town to sell their wares and crafts, or for children who otherwise live and work on the streets. The program serves more than 100 children from 83 families and also provides scholarship opportunities, transitional housing, medical care and a food bank for families in need.

Minimum Requirement: Contact organization for more info.
Cost: Free to volunteer. Volunteers may stay in a guesthouse for $100 per week or $300 per month, breakfast and lunch included.
Based Out Of: San Miguel de Allende

youareanangel@gmail.com
www.casadelosangeles.org

La Gloria English School
Set in Isla de Mujeres, this school aims to empower the local community by giving them the tools they need to work and thrive in an island that continues to gain popularity among tourists. Volunteers can come assist with mentoring the students, help with pronunciation and sit in on classes. Opportunities to teach may arise.

Minimum Requirement: None. Volunteers can visit a class for one day.
Cost: Free
Based Out Of: Isla de Mujeres

lagloria@gmail.com
www.folges.org

.... **HUMAN RIGHTS AND ADVANCEMENT** ....

Fundación En Vía
En Vía provides interest-free micro-loans to help women in Oaxaca start or expand their small businesses. Funds are gathered by tours, which visit the borrowers and their businesses, and also help to provide free English and business classes to the women after the loans have been paid back. Volunteers typically work as English teachers, program managers, business coordinators, or volunteer coordinators.

Minimum Requirement: 1 month
Cost: Free, volunteers cover their own living and transportation costs

Based Out Of: Oaxaca City

+011 52 951-515-2424
info@envia.org
www.envia.org

SiKanda

SiKanda works towards creating a more just world for all with social and economic programs that help to eradicate poverty and improve living conditions. Volunteers are encouraged to bring their own skills to the table and support SiKanda in a variety of ways, from working on an ongoing social project to assisting with fundraising and graphic design.

Minimum Requirement: Short-term and long-term volunteer projects available.
Cost: Free, volunteer cover own expenses
Based Out Of: Oaxaca

+011 52 195-120-14992
info@si-kanda.org
www.si-kanda.org

Tsomanotik

Tsomanotik is a group dedicated to agricultural and environmental awareness and protection. They live and work on an agroecological center in Chiapas that practices sustainability and educates the local community about sustainable practices. Volunteers assist with eco projects and also support with outreach and education.

Minimum Requirement: 1 week
Cost: Free
Based Out Of: Tzimol, Chiapas

www.manotik.org

ANIMALS

Grupo Ecológico de la Costa Verde

Grupo Ecologico is the first environmental non-profit to work in the protection of sea turtles and has been recognized officially as such from the Mexican government. The group aims to gather information and protect sea turtles, marine life and the environment, in addition to helping improve the development of coastal communities through education, clean-up campaigns, and programs to ensure public health and welfare.

Minimum Requirement: 2 months
Cost: Volunteers pay $250 a month in lodging and are responsible for their own expenses. Grupo Ecologico works to provide housing and volunteers typically share a house.
Based Out Of: San Francisco, 32 miles north of Puerto Vallarta

311-258-4100
From the USA: +011 52 311-258-4100
grupo-eco@project-tortuga.org
www.project-tortuga.org

Photo courtesy of Michael Pettet

FOOD & RECIPES

*– recipes provided by **Chef Ruth Alegria***

Basic Limonada
(Agua de limón)

For each serving you'll need:
1 cup water
1 lime, both juice and rind (note that Mexican limes tend to be slightly smaller than the size of golf balls)
2 tbs. sugar, or to taste

Peel a little less than half the rind off of each lime. Be careful not to include the white parts, which make the limonada bitter. Cut the limes into quarters and blend with water and sugar, for about five seconds. Don't purée the limes completely—you want chunks of lime left over. Longer blending will result in bitterness rather than the sweet-tart flavor the drink should have. Pour the contents of the blender through a strainer into the serving pitcher or individual glasses.

Interested in learning how to cook authentic Mexican? Ruth offers some pretty amazing cooking classes in Mexico City. Email ruthalegria@mac.com or visit *www.mexicosoulandessance.com* for more information.

Cucumber Lemonade with Chia Seeds
(Agua de Pepino con Chia)

1 cucumber, peeled and cubed, with seeds
1 lime, or more to taste
5 cups water
sugar to taste
5 tsp. chia seeds

Add cucumber and water to a blender and purée. Strain into a pitcher. Add lime juice to taste, and sugar. Sprinkle in chia seeds. Serve over ice.

Tomatillo Salsa with Chile de Arbol

1/2 lb. tomatillos
5 or 6 chiles de árbol,
1 clove of garlic
salt to taste
2 tbs. water

Roast the first three ingredients.
Place garlic and chiles into a blender. Blend the mixture until smooth. Add the tomatillos. Blend the salsa until it is slightly chunky. Add salt to taste and serve.

Chipotle Sauce

In a skillet, heat oil and fry the chipotles until they darken.
Put the fried chipotles into the hot water, off of the flame.
In the same skillet, fry canela and cloves, remove when fragrant. Keep the oil.

In a blender, add all the ingredients and liquify. Return to the skillet and fry, stirring constantly for a minimum of 10 minutes up to 20 minutes.

Salsa Molcajeteada

The archetypal Mexican salsa - the ingredients are first roasted and then ground to a rough consistency in a molecajete. And of course there are as many variations as there are home cooks. Depending on the size of your molecajete you can adjust the amounts of the ingredients.

4 Roma tomatoes
1 to 2 jalapeno or serrano peppers
1 garlic clove
salt to taste

Roast the first four ingredients until blistered and charred. Have a bowl with a small amount of cold water ready for your ingredients. Let them cool down and then beginning with the chiles, grind them in your molecajete adding salt and water as necessary. You can add raw, finely chopped onion and cilantro when serving with roasted meats.

Grilled Cactus Orange and Red Onion Salad

In Mexico City, vendors sell cactus paddles that are already cleaned, with spines removed. They sell various sizes, but the smallest are the most tender and flavorful. This dish is very easy to prepare and can be done in a skillet, or over a grill.

12 tender young cactus paddles, spines removed, and washed
12 spring onions or large-bulb scallions, washed
Small amount of oil
Salt and white pepper

Optional
2 medium sized oranges cut into supremes
1/2 red onion sliced thinly
2 tbs. olive oil, 1 tbs. lime juice salt and white pepper for dressing

First, check that all spines have been removed. Rinse and dry the nopal for grilling. Leaving the root end intact, score each cactus paddle with a sharp knife. Heat dry skillet or griddle over high heat. Brush paddles with oil and grill until tender, and paddles have changed from a bright to dull green color. Add spring onions to the skillet as well and cook until charred. Season cactus and onions with dressing. Remove to serving platter.

Mole de Olla Meat and Vegetable Stew

Ancho and pasilla chiles give this stew its deep color and rich flavor. It can be made with pork neck bones or boiling beef (brisket/shoulder/short ribs). Use bones for a deeper flavor in the broth.

For the meat:
2 quarts water
3 lbs. stewing beef or pork, cut into 1-inch cubes
Salt to taste
Chiles for seasoning
4 ancho chiles, stemmed and seeded
4 guajillo or pasilla chiles, stemmed and seeded
1 lb. tomatillos, husked (*asado en comal* or simmer for 10 minutes)
1 "sour tuna" *xoconostle* cut in quarters
1 medium onion, chopped
½ head garlic, roughly chopped
pinch of whole cumin seeds
2 tbs. vegetable oil

Vegetables cleaned and trimmed:
4 small zucchini, cut into 1-inch chunks
½ pound green beans, cut in half
8 oz. potatoes peeled and quarted
2 chayotes, peeled and cut into quarters, remove seed
2 ears of corn, each cut into quarters
3 sprigs epazote

Cover the meat with water, bring to a boil, reduce heat, and simmer, covered, until the beef is tender, about 1 hour. When the beef is cooked, strain the broth, reserving the broth and the beef. Roast the chiles. Place them in a saucepan with the *xoconostle*, tomatillos, garlic, onion, cumin ground until the chiles soften, 2-5 minutes.

Place this mixture in a blender and puree until smooth. Heat the oil in a saucepan, add the puree into the hot oil and cook over medium low heat, stirring for about 5 to 10 minutes to desired consistency. Add to the meat and its broth.

Add the vegetables when the meat is fork tender and cook for another 30 minutes.

Add the epazote last, about 5 minutes before the mole is ready to serve.

Serve with hot tortillas, lime wedges, and finely chopped white onion.

························· CHILES ·························

Dried Chile Ancho
Its color is a *"cafe rojizo"* or reddish coffee. Its length about 5 inches (12 cm.), at its widest about 3 inches (7 cm.) Wrinkled skin, shiny appearance, with a triangular shape. They should be flexible and never rigid. When wet, its color is brick red. When purchasing, hold up to the light, the color should be reddish. Fresh it is the Chile Poblano.

Do not confuse with the chile mulato, which is larger, darker and coffee colored.

Dried Pasilla
Long (pasilla means large) also known as chile negro for its black skin. It has a shiny surface puckered with vertical ridges.

Chile Pasillo
Its color is a *"cafe negruzco"* or dark coffee. Its length about 6 inches to 8 inches (15 to 20 cm). Its skin is shiny and wrinkled. Piquant in taste. Fresh it is the Chile Chilaca.

Cascabel Chipotle Mulato

Puya

Chilhaucle

Guajillo

Ancho New Mexico

Pasilla

tortas

- Jamón y queso $18
- De pierna   25
- De Pollo   25
- Especial   30
  (pierna ó pollo, jamón y queso)

Hamburguesas

- Sencilla $25
- Especial   30
  (carne, jamón y queso)

Sandwich

- con jamón $16
  y Queso
- con Atún   18
- con Pechuga de   22
  Pavo
- con Pechuga de   22
  Pollo
- con pierna   25
- Especial
  (pierna, jamón y queso)

Licuados con

* Fresa
* Guaraba
* Papaya
* Melón
* Platano
* Manzana

*elige tu Comb

Quesadillas

- Sencilla $10
- con jamon   13
- con champiñon   15
- con Pechuga   18
  de Pavo
- Pollo   18
- ...erna   18
- ...rachera   20

Baguets

- con Arrachera $35
  (Arrachera y champiñon)
- con Pollo   35
  (Pollo y champiñon)
- Especial   40
  (Arrachera ó pollo, champiñones,
  Jamón y queso)

Ensaladas

- ensalada $35
  cesar con pollo
- ensalada cesar $40
  con pollo y tocino

Jugos Natu

* Naranja
* Toronja
* Zanahoria
* betabel
* Jugo Hierr...
  (Naranja, betabel, Apio...)
* Jugo Quema...
  (Piña, Apio, Perejil, Lim...)
* Jugo Colest...
  (Naranja, Nopal, Apio...)

A BREAKDOWN OF COMMON MEXICAN CUISINE

Agua Fresca
Fresh fruit blended with water; sometimes sugar is added. Every restaurant and street food stand will offer a fresh fruit juice of the day. Our favorite was hibiscus water, or *agua de jamaica*.

Ceviche
Popular along both coasts, *ceviche* is fresh, raw fish (usually the catch of the day) marinated in lime juice with added chiles and raw vegetables. Commonly eaten on a crunchy tostada with hot sauce.

Chicharron
Fried pork skin

Chile Relleno
Stuffed green chiles. Chiles are roasted and stuffed with cheese, then fried and topped with salsa.

Churros
Fried pastry, coated with cinnamon and sugar. They are usually made to order, and delicious with hot chocolate or coffee.

Cielo Rojo/Michelada
There are millions of variations of these drinks, but it's usually a mixture of lime, salt, spices, hot sauce and beer. *Cielo rojo* also includes clamato juice. You're going to want one after a night out on the town!

Conchas
Sweet bread. Resembles a seashell and comes in various flavors. Great with coffee.

Enchiladas
Corn tortilla that is stuffed and rolled, then topped with chile sauce and baked. Fillings vary, but almost always include cheese.

Flan
Traditional Mexican dessert. The texture is similar to custard. Made with sugar, eggs, condensed and evaporated milk and flavor (vanilla or chocolate).

Flor de Calabaza
Squash blossoms, usually wilted and cooked with cheese inside a tortilla. *Flor de Calabaza* quesadillas are common in Mexico City.

Horchata
A traditional drink made of rice, almonds and cinnamon, and sweetened with sugar. It looks like milk, but is dairy-free (and delicious).

Huarache
Fried masa in the shape of a huarache sandal, and topped with salsa, onions, potato, cilantro, protein and cheese.

Huitlacoche
Corn truffle, commonly found in quesadillas. Also known as the "Mexican truffle."

Masa
Corn dough.

Mezcal
Distilled alcohol made from maguey. Tastes like very strong tequila.

Mole
Traditional in Oaxaca and Puebla, mole is a sauce. Recipes vary, but always contain chile and many spices, and if it's brown, chocolate. Usually served over meat.

Pulque
Fermented alcoholic beverage. Dates back to the Mayan times. Common in Mexico City.

Quesadilla
Flour or corn tortillas served with melted cheese in the center.

Raicilla
Mexican moonshine. Similar to mezcal and tequila, but much stronger in flavor.

Tamale or Tamal
Masa stuffed with meat, cheese, vegetables or fruit, wrapped in a corn husk or banana leaf and steamed or boiled. Tamales usually contain lard.

Tlayuda
One very large tostada topped with beans, guacamole, salsa, cheese, lettuce and protein. Typical Oaxacan street food.

Torta
Sandwich

Tortillas
Similar to flat bread. Base is either corn or flour.

EATING VEGETARIAN OR VEGAN IN MEXICO

If you're a vegetarian traveling through Mexico, you'll probably be surprised by how much there is to eat. You definitely won't starve, but you may get burned out on beans and rice.

Be aware that many things are cooked with animal products, like lard. Learning how to ask what's in things will come in handy, and this little cheat-sheet will help.

Meat (Carne):
pollo – chicken
mariscos – seafood
pescado or pez – fish
puerco or carne de cerdo – Pork
aves de corral – poultry
pavo – turkey

Animal Products (Productos Animales):
huevos – eggs
leche – milk
lácteos – dairy
queso – cheese
mantequilla – butter
miel – honey
crema – cream
yogurt – yogurt
manteca (de cerdo) – lard
caldo de pollo – chicken broth
mayonesa – mayonnaise
gelatina – gelatin

Other Useful Phrases for Vegetarians and Vegans in Mexico

I am vegan – *Yo soy vegana* (female) / *Yo soy vegano* (male)

I am vegetarian – *Yo soy vegetariano/a*

I don't eat meat. – *Yo no como carne.*

I do not eat meat, pork or chicken. – *Yo no como carne, cerdo/ puerco, ni pollo.*

I (do) (do not) eat eggs, milk/milk products or cheese. – *Yo (como) (no como) huevos, leche/lácteos, o queso.*

I don't eat fish. – *No como pescado.*

I only eat vegetables and fruit. – *Solo como vegetales y fruta.*

Are there some vegetarian restaurants in the city? – *Hay algunos restaurantes vegetarianos en la ciudad?*

How is the rice prepared; with chicken broth, or only with water? – *Como se prepara el arroz; con caldo de pollo, o solamente con agua?*

Soy milk– *leche de soja*

Q&A
MEET A FELLOW TRAVELER

RACHEL LIBERTO
BROOKLYN, NY

Rachel is a female traveler who prefers to travel on her own. We met her on the road in southern Mexico before she crossed the border to Guatemala. Here, she shares why she loves to travel solo and why she plans to return to Mexico in the future.

Why do you travel solo? What's the best thing about it?

I prefer to travel solo. I feel that I get a more authentic experience of the culture and the place when I travel alone. Some of the main advantages to traveling solo are that I am more approachable and less intimidating to local people, I am less distracted by my traveling partner(s) and end up seeing/noticing more. I also love the alone-time reflections that come along with traveling by myself.

What inspired you to visit and work in Mexico and Guatemala?

It's so affordable, beautiful and welcoming.

Did you feel safe traveling on your own through Mexico?

Definitely. Part of my feeling of safety comes from familiarity and from knowing the language but I also don't feel that Mexico is as scary and threatening as people make it out to be. With that said, you should know what places to avoid and the places where you should use more caution traveling alone as a female.

What's crossing the border from Mexico to Guatemala like? Was it safe? Any tips for crossing?

I have crossed the border twice round-trip from San Cristobal de las Casas to Xela (Quetzaltenango). There are two main ways to cross the border from Mexico to Guatemala. One way is to pay for a shuttle ($25–30) and the other way is by public transportation ($11). The shuttle method is easy but no quicker than public transportation. They make a "breakfast" stop at an expensive roadside restaurant for almost an hour in the morning and several other unnecessary rest stops along the way. The public transportation method requires about four transfers but is surprisingly efficient. On average, the trip takes about 6–8 hours, depending on where you are going in Guatemala.

I feel safe taking public transportation. It is helpful to speak Spanish but not necessary. There are a lot of people willing to help you out. Route: collectivo from San Cristobal to Comitan, another collectivo from Comitan to Cuidad Cuauhtemoc (the border). This collectivo will leave you at the Mexican Aduana office (customs). FYI: if you entered Mexico by land and stayed more than 7 days, you will have to pay an exit fee of about 350 pesos. After you pass through Mexican customs, you will grab one of the cabs waiting across the street to the Guatemalan customs office a few miles away in La Mesilla (longest border ever). Once you pass through the Guatemalan customs you can take one of the little red tuk-tuks nearby to the bus terminal. The terminal is walking distance if you don't have too much stuff and don't mind asking directions. From the terminal, you can take a direct bus to several locations in Guatemala or you can take one to a larger town called Huehuetenango, where you can get a bus just about anywhere in the country.

The shuttle route is recommended if the public transportation route seems terrifying to you and/or you don't feel confident in your language and communication skills. It is much simpler but not as exciting. You schedule a shuttle as late as the night before to leave in the morning. The shuttle will take you to the Mexican customs office, wait for the group to get processed, and then it will take you to the Guatemalan customs office. From there, there will be another shuttle to take you to your destination. These shuttles only go to major cities and tourist destinations, so you may have to make other transportation arrangements from these locations if you are going to a more remote area.

What is your biggest challenge traveling through Mexico (and Latin America) as a single woman?

Machismo! It is a challenge for me to be so in love with a culture that is still quite staunchly macho and patriarchal.

What is your favorite thing about Mexico and/or Latin America?

The colors, the delicious and cheap food, the warm and affectionate culture, and the rhythmic, poetic language.

On a scale of 1-10, how important is being able to speak Spanish? Why?

9.5! As a female traveling alone, it will make you feel a whole lot more comfortable and safe if you can understand people and be understood. Speaking the language will also help you make local friends and feel less isolated. It is also best to learn once you are there. Find a language program to kick off your trip with and you will be off to a great start.

Any advice for solo females who want to visit Mexico and continue onto other parts of Central America?

Learn Spanish! And, once you are feeling comfortable and confident, venture off the tourist-path and try to immerse yourself a bit more. Find a homestay, a volunteer project, or visit a more remote area. Trust people and use discretion; most people are not out to get you and you know when you don't feel safe. Respect your own boundaries. You don't have to hide in tourist towns but you also don't need to prove your courage and adventurousness to anyone. If it feels good, do it; if it doesn't feel good, don't do it.

Q&A
MEET A LOCAL

AUREA DENNIS PRADO FLORES, 31
Mexico City, Mexico

Aurea Dennis Prado Flores is a 31-year-old woman who was born and raised in Mexico City. After living in Madrid for six years and traveling through several countries in Europe, she moved back to Mexico—first to Playa del Carmen, Quintana Roo, and later back to Mexico City where she now lives and works on her own.

Do you think Mexico City is safe for a solo female traveler?

As when traveling to all big cities in the world, I think you have to be very careful when visiting Mexico City, even more so if you are alone. México City is very big, but if you follow advice and recommendations, I think you won't have any problems and you can visit the city without many risks. I have been living here almost all my life and fortunately, nothing bad has happened to me.

Do you think machismo is prevalent in modern Mexican society? How so? How does it affect women?

Yes, I think México is still a "machista" society, but it's changing, specifically in México City, because women are different now. We want different things and we are more independent than before, but women still have to fight against machismo sometimes, *like in work situations and even in a relationship with a man.*

We read that many Mexican women live with their families until they get married, and that some get married quite young. Is that still true?

It's true, but it's changing a lot. You can see the change more in México City because it's more cosmopolitan. Now a lot of women are living by themselves and do not get married before their '30s.

What's it like living on your own and working in Mexico City (DF) as a female?

For me it has been a very good experience. México City has everything you need, and in my opinion, if you are used to or ok with living in the biggest city in the world, it can be a very good experience. I haven't had any major problems living on my own or working as a female in DF.

What's dating in Mexico City like? Do guys usually pay on dates, or do you split the bill?

I think dating in México City is not that different from dating in any other countries. Mexican men may be more polite, but it really depends on the guy. Things are changing a lot and now, women pay sometimes too, but some guys are used to paying for everything all the time. If you have a date with a Mexican guy, you can expect to be treated very well. Men here are not as direct as European guys.

What are the best neighborhoods to go out in?

I recommend La Condesa, La Roma, Polanco, the center and Coyoacán.

Any advice for females who plan to visit Mexico City on their own?

First of all, I recommend you stay in a hotel or hostel near downtown, or in the "Condesa" or "Roma" neighborhoods. Those are the most central places, and you can find a lot of things to do there without going very far. You can find places to go out and they are the most cosmopolitan zones of the city. If you know someone in the city or you have some friends, I really recommend staying with them. It is so much better to visit the big city with someone who knows it well.

I also recommend not to go out alone at night, or if you do, staying very close to your hotel or hostel, and always getting a "secure" cab. They are a little more expensive but you don't have any risk in taking them. And finally, you need at least one week to see the big city.

Be sure to visit the historic center, Colonia Roma, Colonia Condesa, Polanco, Chapultepec, Xochimilco, Reforma, and Teotihuacan.

Mexico City is a busy but safe place to live.

Q&A
MEET AN EXPAT

LUCIANA SUAREZ, 26
Sayulita, Nayarit, Mexico

Luciana (Lucy) grew up in Los Angeles, CA, and lived in San Francisco, but when she visited Sayulita seven years ago, she fell in love. She's lived as an expat in Mexico ever since, creating a life for herself in a small beach community on the Pacific coast.

Why did you move to Mexico/Sayulita?

I was in search of a different kind of lifestyle and I was tired of the city life. I fell totally in love with Sayulita. I loved the fact that I could have a place right on the beach and it didn't cost me an arm and a leg. The people are so nice, the food is delicious and fresh, and I liked that I was able to work very little and still make enough money to live a good quality of life.

What made you stay?

I built my home there and I fell in love with someone, and built a really nice life for myself. My family moved down from the States also and became a part of my little Mexican community. And once you go there you'll understand why no one wants to leave.

What are the biggest differences living in Mexico versus the U.S.?

In the States, everything is so accessible and at your fingertips. In Sayulita, since it's a small beach town an hour away from a big city, it makes things that are easy in the U.S. a little more complicated, but it grounds you. Not everyone has access to everything they need all the time in other parts of the world. Figuring that out made me more down to earth.

What's your favorite thing about Mexico?

The people. They're not jaded. They're loving, open, and even if they don't have very many things, they're happy with what they have; being around their family and enjoying every day is enough.

What's been the biggest challenge, living in Mexico?

Getting things done with urgency usually takes a long time in Mexico. Everyone operates on "Mexican time," and things aren't as efficient as in the States. Like if I need a plumber, for example, or someone to fix my car, it's harder to handle. Everything moves at a slower pace in Mexico, and that can be both a good and bad thing.

Do you feel safe there?

Yes I do. I feel safer in Sayulita than I do in downtown L.A. Everyone knows each other and I am not scared to walk alone at night.

What do you think is the biggest misconception of Mexico?

I think a really big misconception has a lot to do with the bad press surrounding the narco-trafficking. People think that the violence is targeted towards tourists, but it's not at all. Mexicans are targeting Mexicans, not foreigners who come to lay on the beach for a week.

What's an average day like in Sayulita?

Without work: Wake up, take an early morning walk on the beach, have a fresh fruit smoothie for breakfast, take the paddle board out for a few hours and swim in the ocean, then tan with friends on the sand and have a few beers. In the afternoon we buy whatever the fresh catch of the day is, make a big ceviche on the beach to share with everyone, go home, have a siesta, and then get ready to go out.

What are Mexican men like to date?

Passionate, chivalrous, romantic, macho, and jealous.

How does machismo affect you?

I am somewhat opinionated and have a strong personality, and sometimes fading in the background is hard for me. But at times I find myself biting my tongue to not hurt someone's ego. Machismo means the man is dominant, and as the woman in a relationship, sometimes I find myself letting the man be right instead of starting a fight over something minor.

What's the best hangover cure?

Cielo rojo—they'll change your life. It's clamato juice, Worcestershire, salsa magi, lime, hot sauce, spices, a cold beer served with a salted rim. Everyone makes theirs differently, but they're always delicious.

Is it easy to go to the gynecologist? Is medicine easy to get?

Yes, completely. And it's affordable. Dentists, doctors and gynecologists are accessible and affordable. Most medicine is over the counter—all you have to do is find a pharmacy. You would think that with it being so accessible, there would be people who have substance abuse problems with prescriptions, but not one person that I know has that problem.

What are three things you need from the states that you can't get in Mexico?

All the deliciousness that comes from Whole Foods, the latest fashions are hard to get, and other random specific cosmetic products.

Any other tips?

When you go to Sayulita, you must: eat at Chile Relleno—it's the most authentic Mexican place, in my opinion. You also must go to Pacha Mama and shop, even if you don't buy anything, and you must learn how to surf—Sayulita is the perfect place for that. Go to Luna Azul and ask for Papas. He's a great instructor.

09 DISTRITO FEDERAL

291-WTF

Ciudad México

TRANSPORTE PARTICULAR AUTOMOVIL

Photo courtesy of Hot Toddies Unlimited.

LANGUAGE

Spanish is very straightforward when it comes to pronunciation. Words are pronounced exactly how they're spelled, and there are very few, if any, exceptions. Start by memorizing vowel sounds:

A = *ahh*

E = *ehh*

I = *eee*

O = *oh*

U = *ooo*

.... COMMON PHRASES ....

Hello: *Hola*

Goodbye: *Adios, chao*

See you later: *Hasta luego*

Yes: *Si*

No: *No*

Please: *Por favor*

Thank you: *Gracias*

Thank you very much: *Muchas gracias*

Excuse me: *Perdon, Disculpa*

Excuse me (as in, can you repeat that?): *Como?*

Where is...?: *Donde esta...?*

Bus Station: *Terminal de omnibus*

Airport: *Aeropuerto*

How much...?: *Cuanto cuesta?*

How can I get there?: *Como puedo llegar?*

I'm sorry: *Lo siento, perdon*

Why?: *Porque?*

Where is the bathroom?: *Donde esta el bano?*

Left: *Izquierda*

Right: *Derecha*

Straight: *Derecho*

I need help: *Necesito ayuda*

Let's Go: *Vamonos*

Ashtray: *Sinisero*

Tip: *Propina*

SHOPPING

Can you help me please?: *Me puede ayudar por favor?*

Can you discount this?: *Puede ser menos? Hay discuento?*

I'm just looking: *Solo estoy mirando*

Do you have something bigger/smaller? *Tienes algo mas grande/chico?*

I'll come back: *Vuelvo/regreso/voy a dar la vuelta*

I like this: *Me gusta*

It's very beautiful: *Es muy bonita*

NUMBERS

0: zero	**14:** catorce	**100:** cien
1: uno	**15:** quince	**200:** doscientos
2: dos	**16:** diez y seis	**300:** trescientos
3: tres	**17:** diez y siete	**400:** cuatrocientos
4: cuatro	**18:** diez y ocho	**500:** quinientos
5: cinco	**19:** diez y nueve	**600:** seiscientos
6: seis	**20:** veinte	**700:** setecientos
7: siete	**30:** treinta	**800:** ochocientos
8: ocho	**40:** cuarenta	**900:** novecientos
9: nueve	**50:** cincuenta	**1000:** mil
10: diez	**60:** sesenta	**2000:** dos mil
11: once	**70:** setenta	**3000:** tres mil
12: doce	**80:** ochenta	**4000:** cuatro mil
13: trece	**90:** noventa	...And so on

GENERAL RULE FOR NUMBERS BELOW 100

21: *twenty + 1 = veinte y uno*

46: *forty + 6 = cuarenta y seis*

79: *seventy + 9 = setenta y nueve*

GENERAL RULE FOR NUMBERS ABOVE 100

120: *one hundred + 20 = ciento veinte*

260: *two hundred + 60 = doscientos sesenta*

480: *four hundred + 80 = cuatrocientos ochenta*

RESTAURANTS

Can I have more?: *Puedo tener mas?*

Is it spicy?: *Se pica?*

Plate: *Plato*

It's delicious: *Es muy rico*

May I have a menu?: *Puedo ver la carta?*

I don't eat meat: *No como carne*

I am a vegetarian: *Soy vegetariana*

Can I pay with a credit card?: *Puedo pagar con tarjeta de credito?/Aceptan tarjetas de credito?*

The check, please: *La cuenta, por favor*

With/Add: *Con*

Without: *Sin*

FEELINGS

I like: *Me gusta*

I don't like: *No me gusta*

This is fun: *Es divertido*

I'm hungry: *Tengo hambre*

I'm hot: *Tengo calor/hace calor*

I'm cold: *Tengo frio/hace frio*

I want to go: *Quiero ir*

I'm sick: *Estoy enferma/me siento enferma*

My head hurts: *Duele mi cabeza*

I love Mexico: *Me encanta Mexico*

I miss...: *Extrano...*

SLANG

No mames: *Used to mean no way, or yeah right*

Guey: *Dude*

Chela: *Beer*

Que Onda: *What's up*

Chido/Chevere: *Cool*

Que padre: *How cool*

Un chingo: *A lot*

Pinche: *The f word*

Fuego: *Lighter/Fire*